SACRED SENSE

SACRED SENSE

Discovering the Wonder of
God's Word and World

William P. Brown

WILLIAM B. EERDMANS PUBLISHING COMPANY
GRAND RAPIDS, MICHIGAN / CAMBRIDGE, U.K.

Published 2015 by

Wm. B. Eerdmans Publishing Co.

2140 Oak Industrial Drive N.E., Grand Rapids, Michigan 49505 /

P.O. Box 163, Cambridge CB3 9PU U.K.

Printed in the United States of America

21 20 19 18 17 16 15   7 6 5 4 3 2 1

Library of Congress Cataloging-in-Publication Data

Brown, William P., 1958-
    Sacred sense: discovering the wonder of God's word and world / William P. Brown.
        pages   cm
    Includes index.
    ISBN 978-0-8028-7221-0 (pbk.: alk. paper)
    1. Bible — Criticism, interpretation, etc.   2. Wonder.   3. Awe.   I. Title.

    BS511.3.B76   2015
    220.6 — dc23

                                                        2015005611

www.eerdmans.com

Contents

Preface and Acknowledgements

This may very well be the hardest book I've ever written, which seems strange to say because I've written much lengthier (and some would say belabored) works over the years. Nevertheless, this has been a particularly challenging book to write, but not because it has been laborious. To the contrary, it has been a labor of love. Although certain chapters build upon some of my previous work,[1] I've found myself in this book pressed further than I ever expected, lured into uncharted waters guided by currents beyond my control, or at least beyond my once-settled opinions. Writing this book has cultivated a new discipline, the discipline of letting go and seeing what happens.

My area of expertise is biblical studies, specifically the Hebrew Bible or Old Testament, which involves the study of ancient history, ancient artifacts, ancient texts, and ancient languages. Such study, over the years, has enabled me to develop my own translations, as featured in this book. A love for antiquity reigns in this field of study. But my work, particularly this work, is far from antiquarian. I have no desire simply to blow dust off of relics. Instead, I have sought to bring the ancient Scriptures to life and through them to point the reader toward new imaginings, new ways of reading biblical texts, even those texts that remain "dead and buried" in their suffocating familiarity.

---

1. Especially from my *Seven Pillars of Creation: The Bible, Science, and the Ecology of Wonder* (New York: Oxford University Press, 2010); and *Wisdom's Wonder: Character, Creation, and Crisis in the Bible's Wisdom Literature* (Grand Rapids: Eerdmans, 2014).

This is the hardest book because it is the riskiest book I've written. As the reader will soon find out, one of the ways I incorporate wonder in my reading of texts is to pose generative questions sometimes without resolving them, only because they remain unresolved in my own mind, which for a so-called expert is always difficult to admit. But in posing such questions, I have discovered the gift of pondering ambiguities and imagining new possibilities, of reflecting on the mystery to which the text points. And what a blessing that has been!

This book represents my own journey through the Bible, a stumbling attempt to identify what I find most central, most evocative, most wondrous with respect to the Bible's unfolding drama. Were I to take that journey again from Genesis to Revelation (and I will), it would no doubt be different. So expansive and diverse is the biblical landscape that there's always something new to see, always something to be surprised about. This journey, like all journeys, is a highly selective one, and this particular one lingers expectantly where the biblical drama begins and also where it ends, as perhaps every journey through the Bible should do, from creation to new creation. It's what happens in between that becomes quite variable.

This is no academic exercise. References to written works are kept to a relative minimum (at least by scholarly standards). My conversations have taken place more with face-to-face than with eye-to-word or screen-to-screen encounters, in other words, with colleagues in the flesh. I have been blessed to work at Columbia Theological Seminary, a community of partners and pilgrims engaged in this wonderfully odd (and awed) vocation called theological education. They have helped shape my thinking and teaching. I name two in particular: Christine Roy Yoder and Stanley Saunders, with whom I have enjoyed teaching over the years. They were gracious enough to review a couple of chapters when I realized I was stumbling blindly into the unknown. Others include students and former students turned pastors who have read through this or that essay and provided helpful feedback: Kathryn Threadgill, Kate Buckley, and Anna Fulmer. I particularly thank Ralph C. Griffin for his suggested revisions and corrections as he pored over drafts of various chapters in the final stages of revision. In addition, fruitful conversations over the years with colleagues, friends, and neighbors have helped to shape and reshape my thinking along the way: Steve Hayner, Skip Johnson, Stanley Saunders, Christine Roy Yoder, Mark Douglas, Walter Brueggemann, Deborah Mullen, Raj Nadella, Marcia Riggs, Kim Clayton, Rodger Nishioka, Kathy Dawson, Martha Moore-Keish, Brennan Breed, Haruko Ward, Beth Johnson, Kim Long,

David Bartlett, Pamela Cooper-White, Paul Huh, John Azumah, Michael Morgan, Cam Murchison, Erskine Clarke, Bill Harkins, Ralph Watkins, Matthew Fleming, George Stroup, Jeffery Tribble, Rodney Hunter, Carol Newsom, Brent Strawn, Anna Carter Florence, David Florence, and Israel Galindo, among others.

I also want to acknowledge the staff of William B. Eerdmans Publishing Company, particularly Michael Thomson, acquisitions editor, and Jennifer Hoffman, development editor. Both have been a delight to work with. Thanks also to Erskine Clarke, consummate editor and historian, for granting me permission to adapt my sermon "The Ecology of Resurrection," published in *Journal for Preachers* 36.3 (2013): 20-23, as chapter 14.

More personally, I give thanks to my beloved partner Gail, who has provided constant support and inspiration throughout this project and has been a critical reviewer of my writing, draft after draft after draft. And throughout these drafts, our daughters, Ella and Hannah, continue to surprise us as they develop into adults. What a wonder! Thanks also to my parents, Bill and Virginia, for their unflagging support even as they wonder what in the world I'm doing, as do I.

I dedicate this book in memory of my mother-in-law, Mary Deane King (1933-2013), a woman of abundant wonder and countless wonderings. This is the book I wish I had written while she was still alive.

Wonder's Wonder

Wows come in all shapes and sizes, like people.

Anne Lamott[1]

The great Methodist preacher Fred Craddock tells of a practice in which his ancestors would go out walking on Sunday afternoons, sometimes in groups, sometimes alone. They called it "going marveling." On these walks they would admire nature and collect unusual things — from rocks to wild flowers — to bring back home and share to the amazement of others. It was a weekly ritual. Craddock goes on to share an experience of his own:

> When I read that and was reminded of that, I went marveling myself. . . . About a mile away I came upon a pavilion, and inside I saw a lot of people singing, praying, and reading scripture, sharing their love for each other. They were vowing that they would . . . make every effort, God help them, to reproduce the life of Jesus in this place. And I marveled, how I marveled. And I said to myself, *Look what I have found, right here, in this little building.*[2]

---

1. Anne Lamott, *Help, Thanks, Wow: The Three Essential Prayers* (New York: Riverhead, 2012), 74.

2. Fred B. Craddock, *Craddock Stories,* ed. Mike Graves and Richard F. Ward (St. Louis: Chalice, 2001), 65. Many thanks to Kim Clayton for pointing me to this reference.

"Going marveling" is something of a lost practice. Today it could easily be considered a waste of time. But it is something that needs to be retrieved, not only for maintaining physical and mental well-being but also, I submit, for reading Scripture well. The Bible is read and used (and abused) in so many ways: to find answers to pressing questions, prove a point, win an argument, formulate dogma, reconstruct ancient history, get rich, induce shame, and, most tragically, promote violence and justify oppression. For communities of faith, however, there remains a more fundamental, life-giving reason for reading the Bible — to cultivate a sense of wonder about God, the world, others, and ourselves.

Lamentably, whether in Sunday school or in seminary, not much is done in the way of treating Scripture as a source of transforming wonder. This perhaps stems from the overriding tendency to place "belief ahead of wonder," dogma above desire.[3] It is my conviction, in any case, that without wonder at its core, theology ("the study of God") inevitably becomes a rusty relic, a useless language game.[4] Indeed, if there is one central testimony about God throughout the Bible, it is this: *God is encountered in wonder.* One of the earliest testimonies of faith in the Bible comes from the ancient poetry of Exodus 15, which recounts the exodus event:

> Who is like you among the gods, O LORD?
> > Who is like you, majestic in holiness,
> > > praiseworthily awesome, working wonder?[5] (Exod. 15:11)

The divine distinction is rooted in wonder and awe. "You are the God who works wonder," proclaims the psalmist (Ps. 77:14). The "LORD of hosts . . . is wonderful in counsel, excellent in wisdom," proclaims the prophet (Isa. 28:29). The various roles and activities that God performs throughout the Hebrew Bible are deemed exceptionally wondrous: creating, saving, sustaining, protecting, providing, caring, judging, healing, restoring, enlightening, teaching. And one can add the New Testament witness: the crowds marvel at what Jesus does in their midst, from healing to teaching

---

3. Mayra Rivera, "Glory: The First Passion of Theology?" in *Polydoxy: Theology of Multiplicity and Relation,* ed. Catherine Keller and Laurel Schneider (New York: Routledge, 2011), 167-85 at 181.

4. For similarly pointed language, see Karl Barth's chapter on wonder in his *Evangelical Theology: An Introduction* (New York: Holt, Rinehart & Winston, 1963), 63-73.

5. The object is singular *(pele'),* although it is typically translated plural (see New Revised Standard Version and New International Version).

(e.g., Matt. 8:27; 9:33; 21:20; Mark 5:42; Luke 13:17). To witness God's presence and work in the world is first and foremost to marvel.

Without wonder, faith in a God who "works wonder(s)" remains stuck and stagnant. Genuine faith is all about "going marveling" in God's world of wonder. This book attempts to do just that within the world of Scripture: to follow a biblical itinerary of wonder from start to finish. It is my way of saying, "Look what I have found, right here, in this (not so) little book." And what I have found are various "texts of *tremendum*," texts of wonder, a mere sampling of many, many more.

Hunger for Wonder

What is it that makes these particular texts so wondrous? Simply put, they captivate and move me. Such texts find a way of getting under my skin, burrowing into my heart, and drawing me out of myself. They stir my imagination and arouse within me a deep desire to know more, and by "know" I mean more than gaining information or even understanding and insight. These texts evoke an encounter. They arouse within me the yearning to touch and be touched, the desire to know in the fullest sense of knowing, body and soul, sinew and synapse. These are the texts that take my breath away and give breath back to me. They evoke the kind of wonder that leaves me restless and hungry yet hopeful and fulfilled.

"Wonder": although the term covers a wide range of experiences, the common factor is that wonder is naturally desired. We are born with a hunger for wonder firmly rooted in the human psyche. According to bioanthropologist Melvin Konner, the capacity for wonder is "the hallmark of our species and the central feature of the human spirit."[6] Richard Dawkins refers to our "appetite for wonder" as distinctive of the human species.[7] If *Homo sapiens* (the "wise human") is too congratulatory a self-classification, there is no doubt that we are at least *Homo admirans,*

---

6. Melvin Konner, *The Tangled Wing: Biological Constraints on the Human Spirit,* 2nd ed. (New York: Henry Holt, 2002), 488.

7. An appetite that, according to Richard Dawkins, *only* science can fill (*Unweaving the Rainbow: Science, Delusion, and the Appetite for Wonder* [New York: Houghton Mifflin, 1998], 114). I have nothing against science; indeed, I am a strong advocate of scientific investigation and what it contributes to theological reflection. My quibble with Dawkins is his use of the word "only." See William P. Brown, *The Seven Pillars of Creation: The Bible, Science, and the Ecology of Wonder* (New York: Oxford University Press, 2010).

the "wondering human." Not only do we have X and Y chromosomes to determine our genders; we also have what could be called the "Why" chromosome that determines our humanity. The wonder *of* it all prompts one — anyone — to wonder *about* it all. Only humans, as far as we know, can contemplate the mystery of it all, from primordial origin to cosmic purpose. Wonder animates the soul. According to Einstein, "Whoever does not know [mystery] and can no longer wonder, no longer marvel, is as good as dead."[8]

At the conclusion of the great Wesleyan hymn "Love Divine, All Loves Excelling" are the haunting words "lost in wonder, love, and praise." Today, *losing* wonder seems to be more the norm. The reasons are legion. First, we have deluded ourselves into thinking that wonder is reserved exclusively for children. Wonder is something we adults think we must outgrow in order to project confidence, knowledge, and wisdom. (But, as we shall see, wonder has all to do with wisdom!) Moreover, in this age of culture wars, political incivility, racial and religious strife, economic uncertainty, material obsessions, suspicion of the other, and the sheer busyness of life, not to mention our entire planet in peril from environmental abuse, it seems that fear and fatigue have all but replaced love and wonder. And what little is left of our capacity to wonder we have ceded over to the multibillion-dollar entertainment industry. Take it from Einstein: by now we may very well be "as good as dead." Or take it from Rachel Carson: wonder is key to our livelihood on this planet.[9] If we lose our sense of wonder, we consign ourselves and the world to destruction.

The Wonder of Wonder

So what exactly is wonder? It never hurts to begin with the *Oxford English Dictionary,* which devotes several full pages to this one word alone, but it is best summed up in the following words:

> The emotion excited by the perception of something novel and unexpected, or inexplicable; astonishment mingled with perplexity or bewildered curiosity.

8. Albert Einstein, "The World as I See It," trans. Sonja Bargmann, in *Ideas and Opinions, Based on* Mein Weltbild, ed. Carl Seelig (New York: Crown, 1954 [orig. 1931]), 8-11 at 11.
9. Rachel L. Carson, *The Sense of Wonder* (New York: HarperCollins, 1998), 100-101.

At its base, wonder is an emotional response; it cannot be willed into existence. It is a response to something unexpected, and that response reflects a potent mix of curiosity and perplexity. On the one hand, wonder carries the unsettling element of bewilderment. On the other hand, there is the element of insatiable curiosity or the passionate desire to know.[10] Wonder, thus, bears an inner tension.

Celia Deane-Drummond describes two different kinds of wonder. First, wonder can be prompted by experiences that "destabilize the existing order of things,"[11] experiences of disorientation in which the unknown rudely breaks into the world of the familiar, throwing everything into question. Wonder can inspire self-critical introspection, or intense "soul-searching."[12] An experience of wonder, for example, can make us feel small and questioned before the enormity of the new. In such wonder, we are prompted to rethink who we are and our place in the world, and this may entail a whole new outlook — a scary prospect. Wonder can even begin with fear, contrary to popular sanitized versions. Mary-Jane Rubenstein laments that wonder has become sugarcoated in popular usage, connoting only "white bread, lunchbox superheroes, and fifties sitcoms."[13] A deep sense of wonder counters the "prettiness" of superficial understandings that identify wonder only with what is pleasing.[14] Real wonder, on the other hand, can be unsettling. It can embrace the ugly, even the scary. We can be overwhelmed with wonder as easily as we can be incapacitated by fear. Such is the disorienting side of wonder.

The other kind of wonder identified by Deane-Drummond is having a "sense of perfection in the ordering of the world,"[15] a sense of order that

---

10. Historically, curiosity was often seen as antithetical to wonder until the advancement of science beginning in the late sixteenth century. See, most recently, Phillip Ball, *Curiosity: How Science Became Interested in Anything* (Chicago: University of Chicago Press, 2012); Richard Holmes, *The Age of Wonder: How the Romantic Generation Discovered the Beauty and Terror of Science* (New York: Vintage, 2010); and Celia Deane-Drummond, *Wonder and Wisdom: Conversations in Science, Spirituality, and Theology* (Philadelphia: Templeton Foundation, 2006), 1-8.

11. Deane-Drummond, *Wonder and Wisdom,* 1.

12. Cecilia González-Andrieu, *Bridge to Wonder: Art as a Gospel of Beauty* (Waco: Baylor University Press, 2012), 31, 34.

13. Mary-Jane Rubenstein, *Strange Wonder: The Closure of Metaphysics and the Opening of Awe,* Insurrections: Critical Studies in Religion, Politics, and Culture (New York: Columbia University Press, 2008), 10.

14. González-Andrieu, *Bridge to Wonder,* 37.

15. Deane-Drummond, *Wonder and Wisdom,* 2.

invites enthusiastic affirmation, a "yes!" alongside the "wow!" Such wonder comes from discovering a hidden pattern, finding a lost connection, or discerning a haunting melody from a seemingly random arrangement of notes. From the elegance of the universe to the symmetry of snowflakes, this side of wonder is kin to beauty, which can be found equally in mathematics as in music, in art as in astronomy. It is what scientists yearn for, what artists strive for, and what the rest of us enjoy in planetariums, concert halls, galleries, and, perhaps best of all, nature.

Wonder, thus, freely traverses between experiences of order and disorientation, self-critique and celebration, fear and fascination.[16] With such divergence, one might conclude that the notion of wonder is fundamentally incoherent. Not so. Common to all experiences of wonder is their power to attract, immediately or ultimately, rather than to repel.[17] As Abraham Heschel states about wonder's closest sibling, awe: "Unlike fear, [awe] does not make us shrink from the awe-inspiring object, but on the contrary draws us near to it."[18] It is the *affiliative* power of wonder that the *Oxford English Dictionary* associates, quite lamely, with "curiosity." But wonder involves so much more than curiosity. In its fullness, wonder "stops us dead," as it were, in our mindless routines, shattering our "illusion of control and omnipotence,"[19] while at the same time arousing our desire to venture forth in a new direction. Wonder may begin with the push of fear, but it ultimately draws us into its embrace. In wonder, fascination overcomes fear, desire overtakes dread. The arousal of desire, in fact, captures well wonder's affiliative power: wonder awakens desire, and with desire a new attentiveness is born, a freshness of perception that "imbues the world with a certain 'luring' quality."[20] Wonder draws us forward; it beckons us while "shattering our

---

16. It is no accident that wonder's double-sidedness parallels Rudolf Otto's famous notion of the "holy," which he described as *mysterium tremendum et fascinans,* an experience of mystery characterized by both fear and fascination; *The Idea of the Holy: An Inquiry into the Non-rational Factor in the Idea of the Divine and Its Relation to the Rational* (New York: Oxford University Press, 1958), 12-40. This generative dialectic, however, is by no means limited to the experience of the divine, as I hope to show.

17. Robert C. Fuller, *Wonder: From Emotion to Spirituality* (Chapel Hill: University of North Carolina Press, 2006), 60.

18. Abraham Joshua Heschel, *God in Search of Man: A Philosophy of Judaism* (New York: Farrar, Straus & Giroux, 1955), 77.

19. González-Andrieu, *Bridge to Wonder,* 36.

20. Fuller, *Wonder,* 66.

preconceptions, disclosing new possibilities, and revealing previously unknown dimensions of reality."[21]

For all its power to move us, to touch us body and soul, is wonder something that can be analyzed or categorized? Sam Keen, in a now classic study, identifies three basic kinds of wonder: (1) ontological wonder, (2) sensational wonder, and (3) mundane wonder.[22] The first marvels that there are facts at all, that there is something rather than nothing, being rather than nothingness. Whether you are an atheist or a pietist, think about it hard enough and you will inevitably be gripped with wonder. Sensational wonder, to put it in contemporary terms, has its "wow factor." It is the blockbuster kind of wonder that Hollywood loves to conjure every summer, but it is more deeply felt when seeing the Grand Canyon or Iguazu Falls for the first time (and anytime thereafter). Each of the "seven wonders of the world," whether ancient or modern, natural or constructed, has its "wow factor." Mundane wonder, by contrast, is wonder elicited by small, familiar things, such as a baby's smile, an affectionate touch, or a good night's sleep. Things we take for granted or consider ordinary become charged with new meaning; they are experienced differently. Wonder is the familiar becoming new and fresh or downright strange.

There may well be other kinds of wonder (see the subsequent chapters), but regardless of category, wonder is at root relational because it is all about encounter. It is as if the object or source of wonder reaches out and grabs us, shakes us, puzzles us, disturbs us, or embraces us (or all of the above). Wonder draws us in. We sense in wonder a new connection within ourselves to something beyond ourselves, whether it is a *wow!* or an *ahh!* or a *hmmmm.* Wonder adds a touch of surprise, if not mystery, to our lives. The more profound the wonder, the more we lose ourselves in it, and the more we lose ourselves in wonder, the more profound it becomes.

Profound wonder propels us toward the unknown and at the same time arouses our desire to know amid the unknown.[23] There is an insatiable quality to wonder,[24] and knowing with wonder is a special kind of know-

21. Kelly Bulkeley, *The Wondering Brain: Thinking about Religion with and beyond Cognitive Neuroscience* (New York: Routledge, 2005), 17.

22. Sam Keen, *Apology for Wonder* (New York: Harper & Row, 1969), 22-23. For clarity's sake, I am separating out "sensational" from "mundane," which Keen curiously subsumes under "mundane."

23. Jerome A. Miller, *In the Throe of Wonder: Intimations of the Sacred in a Post-Modern World* (Albany: SUNY Press, 1992), 130.

24. Keen, *Apology for Wonder,* 22.

ing. In wonder the object of knowing never becomes conquered territory or something consumed. To know something in wonder is to participate rather than to appropriate; it is to be awakened and made vulnerable, transformed in an ongoing adventure of knowing. In wonder, mystery remains, but it remains ever alluring, drawing us into greater awareness. Wonder is prompted by something or someone quintessentially *other,* wholly outside of us yet striking a resonant chord deep within us. Wonder is being touched by *otherness,* and it requires becoming vulnerable to the source or object of wonder.[25] Whether in beauty or in ugliness, the experience of wonder comes unbidden, as a disruption and, ultimately, as a gift.

Yes, wonder is akin to mystery, but it is far from ignorance, blissful or otherwise. Philosophers, both ancient and modern, have identified wonder's luring yet perplexing character as the very basis of deep inquiry. Socrates famously claimed that "wonder [*to thaumazein*] is the only beginning of philosophy," the love of wisdom.[26] Put more provocatively, wonder is "surrendering ourselves to the *eros* of inquiry."[27] It is both wonder's gravitational pull and its "frightening indeterminacy" that keeps the pursuit of wisdom ever ongoing, ever generative and open to the new.[28]

Wonder, thus, is a paradox: it instills a reverent, even fearful, receptivity toward the other, a posture of standing back or bending the knee. Such is wonder's affinity with awe. At the same time, wonder quickens the desire to venture forth, toward the source or object of wonder. Wonder kindles the "*eros* of inquiry," the desire to know intimately but never fully, for the full satisfaction of desire entails, paradoxically, the death of desire. Wonder cultivates an emotional and cognitive openness that is genuinely receptive yet ever restless. Such are the two sides of wonder: awe and inquiry. Born of awe, wonder is ultimately more active than awe. Wonder animates: "In wonder I want to leap or run, in awe to kneel."[29]

25. Serene Jones, *Trauma and Grace: Theology in a Ruptured World* (Louisville: Westminster John Knox, 2009), 163.

26. *Theaetetus* 155d, in Plato, *Theaetetus, Sophist,* trans. Harold North Fowler, Loeb Classical Library (Cambridge: Harvard University Press, 1967), 54-55.

27. Miller, *In the Throe of Wonder,* 15, 53.

28. Rubenstein, *Strange Wonder,* 7. For the mutual relationship between wonder and wisdom, see William P. Brown, *Wisdom's Wonder: Character, Creation, and Crisis in the Bible's Wisdom Literature* (Grand Rapids: Eerdmans, 2014).

29. Martha C. Nussbaum, *Upheavals of Thought: The Intelligence of Emotions* (New York: Cambridge University Press, 2001), 54n53.

Fear Seeking Understanding

Wonder's paradoxical nature can be found in the Hebrew Scriptures. For the biblical sages wonder has much to do with "the fear of the LORD." The biblical writers claimed a peculiar kind of fear, a fear that draws one to God, not causes one to withdraw from God (contra Gen. 3:8). The "fear of the LORD," in other words, is an *affiliative* fear, which seems oxymoronic because we think of fear only as an avoidance response: flight or fight. But the sages and psalmists of Scripture discerned a different kind of fear, a fear that trembles at the threshold of approach, not flees through the exit door.

From Psalm 111:10 comes the oft-quoted line: "The fear of the LORD is the beginning of wisdom" (cf. Prov. 1:7; 9:10). There, God is praised for doing "great works" and "wonderful deeds," for providing food, for keeping covenant, for doing justice, for redeeming people, for being gracious and merciful. Those are the reasons, according to the psalmist, for "fearing the LORD," and such "fear" is expressed in praise and delight. "Great are the works of the LORD, studied by all who delight in them" (Ps. 111:2). Or as Karl Barth, the great Swiss theologian, noted in a sermon he preached in the Prison of Basel in 1958, the fear of God is "inspired with secret jubilation and is born of gratitude."[30] What a strange fear this is! Such fear, the biblical sages claim, is foundational to wisdom (Prov. 1:7). Call it "fear seeking understanding," or "inquisitive awe." Or simply wonder.[31]

The Unifying Scope of Wonder

But wonder extends far beyond the Bible. One could claim that the entire progress of science, from Francis Bacon to Lynn Margulis and Stephen Hawking, has been driven by an insatiable sense of wonder about the natural realm. Science is fundamentally the search for elegance and order in the physical world, the search for patterns, whether cosmological or biological.[32] Wonder, moreover, is foundational to various modes of human

---

30. Karl Barth, "The Fear of the Lord Is the Beginning of Wisdom," *Interpretation* 14 (1960): 433-39 at 438.

31. For further detail, see Brown, *Wisdom's Wonder,* 24, 37-38.

32. See, e.g., Mary Bruce Campbell, *Wonder and Science: Imagining Worlds in Early Modern Europe* (Ithaca: Cornell University Press, 1999); and Lorraine Daston and Katherine Park, *Wonders and the Order of Nature* (New York: Zone, 1998), esp. 303-28.

expression, such as art and poetry. "Poetry is the official palace language of Wow," notes Anne Lamott.[33] And as for art and music,

> What can we say beyond Wow, in the presence of glorious art, in music so magnificent that it can't have originated solely on this side of things? . . . We stand before Monet and Rothko and the Sphinx and Georgia O'Keefe and are speechless, in awe. Awe is why we are here.[34]

Is it, then, too far a stretch to claim that what art and science share in common is wonder? Wonder, according to astrobiologist Chris Impey, is the "vital spark . . . that drives the best science."[35] The experience of wonder or mystery, according to Albert Einstein, "stands at the cradle of true art and true science." Hence, the iconic Venn diagram.[36]

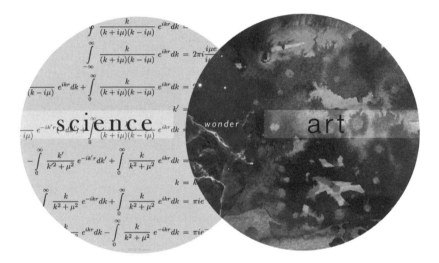

If this is true, then a third overlapping circle should be added. Call it faith or religion. If wonder is what drives good science, if wonder is what inspires great art, perhaps wonder also lies at the heart of biblical faith. Such is my thesis.

33. Lamott, *Help, Thanks, Wow*, 79.

34. Lamott, *Help, Thanks, Wow*, 81, 83.

35. Chris Impey, *The Living Cosmos: Our Search for Life in the Universe* (New York: Random, 2007), 212.

36. Image accessed 4 April 2014 at http://www.brainpickings.org/index.php/2012/02/23/systematic-wonder/.

Reading with Wonder: A Textual Orientation

Taking up the task of filling in the missing circle, this book is about reading Scripture with an eye for wonder. It is a strange discipline, but then the Bible is a strange book as far as religious texts go. The Bible did not drop down from heaven on golden plates, nor was it dictated to an illiterate prophet in the course of a few years. No, the Bible is the product of centuries upon centuries of struggle for understanding and discernment, a vast repository of wonderings and insights regarding God's presence and work in the world, all from communities that were largely oppressed and occupied by the dominant powers of the day. For all its lengthy development and historical coverage, the Bible is itself a wonder, wondrously full of all kinds of discourse: dramatic narrative, love poetry, philosophical musings, moral instruction, jurisprudence, riddles, proverbs, parables, praise, and lament. Overall, the Bible prefers stories over systems, poetry over treatise, prayer over creed. Reading with wonder is reading not for information (how do you do that with love poetry?) or even for answers to urgent questions. It is not a means toward a specific end, not with some useful purpose in mind. It is the kind of reading that lingers; it is reading with keen attentiveness, savoring every word and detail. It is reading with readiness for surprise and in the process raising "wonderings" — questions and ponderings that stir the imagination and generate thinking, without leading necessarily to one way of understanding the text. Reading with wonder revels in generative possibilities. Reading with wonder is responding with wonder. It is marveling at the open mystery to which the text points.

Because wonder is ambiguous by nature, reading with wonder is at ease with ambiguity and easily accommodates multiple perspectives. Reading with wonder shies away from leapfrogging toward a specific resolution or a single answer to a quandary. It is a way of abiding in the text while also bumping around within it, feeling the text's jagged contours, peering into its dark crevices, looking for anomalies and subtleties that raise eyebrows as well as, on occasion, the hair on the back of the neck. In wonder, the text provides space for wondering. As wonder quickens the mind and the heart, so reading with wonder requires both emotional and cognitive investment (which are, in fact, inseparably related). Reading with wonder requires a resolutely singular focus on a text whose meaning is never fixed or static. As the reader is no passive object, so neither is the text in the eye (and ear) of the beholder. When a tree falls in the forest without anyone to hear it, does it make a sound?[37] When a book falls open from the shelf but without anyone to read it, does it convey meaning? No. The text comes alive only when it is read, only when it is heard, or whenever it is remembered. Otherwise, the text is merely marks on a page or pixels on a screen. In wonder, not only does the text fall open to the reader, the reader falls open to the text, come what may. While the interpretive relationship forged between a particular text and a particular reader is unique and ever evolving, it is a relationship that is also meant to be shared in dialogue with other readers. Wonder inspires sharing.

Reading with wonder also recognizes that no text is a solitary object. A text is always read in dialogue, consciously or unconsciously, with other texts in other contexts, and the connections discerned among them can give pause for wonder, even moments of *eureka!* And as no text is an island, so the reader is no isolated subject. She or he navigates a multilayered network of relationships that influence the way texts are read and understood. This is no detriment. Reading with wonder most powerfully takes place in communion with others, in which new questions are raised, fresh insights are shared, and, most importantly, new relationships are formed. Reading with wonder broadens and deepens the community of readers.

In the act of reading, the world of the biblical text becomes part of the reader's world, which itself is a multiverse of various contexts (cultural, psychological, intellectual, ecclesiological, etc.) that shape the world shared between text and reader. Navigating these worlds as one reads the text is itself an adventure, an exercise in wonder. Bringing together disparate worlds or contexts into dialogue, such as biblical poetry and modern science, can yield surprising and often wondrous results.[38] When the speaker in Psalm 139, for example, declares herself to be "wonderfully and fearfully" made (139:14), knowing something about human anatomy, including the marvelous complexity of the brain with its 85 billion neurons and the 100 trillion microbes that reside inside and on each one of us, only increases a sense of awe regarding our created bodies. Equally so is when the psalmist is awestruck before the night sky and declares, "When I look at your heavens, the work of your fingers, the moon and the stars that you have established . . ." (8:3). Far exceeding what the ancient psalmist knew, our knowledge of the universe with its 100 billion galaxies, each with its

---

37. Yes, but only if "sound" is defined as the vibration of air molecules without reference to a hearing subject.

38. By way of illustration, see Brown, *Seven Pillars of Creation*.

100 billion stars or so, only deepens the amazement the speaker must have felt and presses the wonder of humanity's identity and place in creation all the more (8:4).

The wonder of a text is also found in the "big picture" the text conjures in the reader's imagination. A slow, careful reading can sometimes get mired in the textual details and thereby miss the forest for the trees. This is not to say that detailed analysis is at fault. To the contrary, a close reading of the text is essential in discovering the text's novel subtleties and surprising twists. But that is only half the story. The reader must also step back and consider the text as a whole and what it conjures as a whole, just like observing a painting from a certain distance to gain greater clarity. It is one thing to study the brush strokes; it is another to behold the larger image that emerges from the canvas.

Speaking of image, biblical texts revel in imagery, including metaphor. Ancient texts evoke as much as they claim. To linger over their words is to visualize the images they conjure, metaphors that stimulate reflection, reshape our perceptions, and even inspire action. Such images reorient the way we see things and thus the way we relate to them. Such is the power of the image, a fact that commercial media experts know and exploit all too well. But for the ancients, it was primarily the spoken word that did the heavy lifting. In the ear and out the eye, heard and visualized.

Reading Scripture with wonder requires an openness to seeing, hearing, smelling, tasting, and touching something new. Through its evocative use of language, the Bible engages the full range of the senses. Scripture is a full-bodied text that requires full-bodied engagement. "Taste and see that the LORD is good," invites the psalmist (34:8). Taste and see that these words are wondrous and true, I invite the reader (Ezek. 3:1-3). For Christians, the words of Scripture point ultimately to the "Word made flesh," the embodied, incarnate, enfaced Word. The verbal word reflects the bodily Word. Such a wonder! It is no coincidence that wonder works when it is fully felt, fully embodied, a sense that involves the senses.

Reading the Bible with wonder inspires passion: passion for God, passion for community, passion for life and for all that makes life whole and good. Such passion draws one out of the shell of defensiveness and takes one away from survival mode and into common-life mode. Bible-inspired wonder is what drives many to commit themselves to lives of justice and mercy, wisdom and hope, joy and perseverance, charity and responsibility. To borrow from Judaism, such passion leads to *tikkun olam,* to "repairing the world," or put another way, to a life of self-giving love for the world.

Texts of *Tremendum*

The texts selected here cover the gamut of wonder's wide range. Wonder wears many faces in the Bible, from the "fear of the LORD" to the beauty of creation, from Wisdom's delight to the cross of Christ. These texts do more than simply recount certain wondrous encounters; they attempt through word and imagery to (re)create something of an experience of wonder, to share it, to kindle the reader's imagination and desire. These texts facilitate encounters. It is no wonder, then, that many are poetic, for poetry is the official language of mystery. But whether as prose or as poetry, such texts aim to draw the reader in and take the reader to the threshold of the Other.

These "texts of *tremendum*," as I call them, require unhurried inquiry. Speed reading a text of *tremendum* is like trying to sprint through waist-high water: you do so at your frustration, if not peril. Each text is thick with meaning and thin with transparency that points beyond itself. Each has its own symbolic background that requires careful unpacking. Reading these texts is like learning a new language. Without the necessary work of decoding, these texts may otherwise strike the reader as confusing rather than illuminating, pointless rather than profound, or simply confirming what one already thinks or knows. The text evokes its strange wonder only if there is some understanding of its rich background: its historical and literary settings, its dialogue partners and rhetorical aims, in other words the text's "otherness." Such is one task of this book.

But it is not the only task. To glimpse the world *behind* the text merely sets the stage for entering the world *of* the text, a "strange new world" (with apologies to Karl Barth). The task at hand is to read texts — some familiar, others unfamiliar — in ways that recapture their wondrous surprises, both unsettling and insightful, all of which remain hidden from the eye of the beholder who thinks he has seen it all.

1. *Cosmic Wonder*

GENESIS 1:1–2:3

Then God said, "Let light be!"

Genesis 1:3

Given its pride of place, Genesis 1:1–2:3 (hereafter Genesis 1) serves as the official gateway to the Bible, a towering, majestic entrance into all of Scripture. Put to music, Genesis 1 would be something like a Bach organ fugue, full of contrapuntal variations filling every nook and cranny of a Gothic cathedral. But instead of resounding notes, we hear divinely spoken cadences reverberating throughout an intricately ordered universe.

One of the many but overlooked wonders of Genesis 1 is its mathematical intricacy. The account is crafted around seven days, eight acts, and ten commands. As the number ten matches the number of commandments in the Decalogue (Exod. 20:2-17; 34:28), so the number seven is no random counting. God "saw" and pronounced creation "good" seven times; "earth" or "land" (same word in Hebrew) appears twenty-one times; the word "God" is repeated thirty-five times. The number seven, and multiples thereof, is also attested in certain sections in Genesis 1. The first verse consists of seven words; the second contains fourteen. The final section, Genesis 2:1-3, yields a count of thirty-five. And the total word count of the account in Hebrew is 469 or 7 × 67. Genesis 1 is a numerologist's wonderland. One could go on, but the most obvious example is no doubt the most important: the seventh day marks the climax of the account, the only day declared "holy." The number seven connotes a sense of completion, of

15

mission accomplished and order achieved. By numerical reckoning alone, Sabbath, one could say, is the solution to the equation of creation.

It is no coincidence that Genesis 1 is the most complex, intricately structured text of the entire Bible. It is, one could say, the brain of the Bible. Given its head position in the canon, Genesis 1 determines how the rest of Scripture is to be understood, subsuming everything that follows under the God who created "in the beginning." Everything that follows Genesis 1 is infused with cosmic, creational significance, from the emancipation of Israelite slaves to the cry of dereliction on the cross, from a burning bush to broken bread. So also the Apocalypse.

Genesis 1 is also the Bible's closest thing to a "natural" account of creation.[1] Compared to the gripping (and gory) drama of the Babylonian creation myth *(Enuma elish),*[2] Genesis 1 reads like a dry, dense treatise. Rigorously methodical in its presentation, the Bible's opening chapter resembles more an itemized list than a flowing narrative. Genesis 1 is a highly disciplined text, reflecting a literary austerity that scrupulously avoids the wholly unnecessary drama of epic conflict. The text's literary restraint is itself a mark of wonder.

Historical Context

There is, however, a great deal of drama lurking beneath the text's intricate surface. Written most likely near the end of, or soon after, Israel's exile in Babylon in the sixth century B.C.E., Genesis 1 offers a cosmic vision for a community intent on rebuilding itself from the ground up. The Babylonian exile of 587 B.C.E. had left the land of Judah decimated. From the perspective of those most affected, conquest and deportation rendered their land "formless and void" (Gen. 1:2). The survivors experienced this national trauma as nothing less than a cosmic upheaval that left the land emptied of life as they knew it, with the temple lying in ruins, much of Jerusalem razed to the ground, and the community thus stripped of its national and religious identity. Many came to think of their God as a loser, soundly

---

1. For a detailed comparison between the creation perspective of Gen. 1 and scientific cosmology, see William P. Brown, *The Seven Pillars of Creation: The Bible, Science, and the Ecology of Wonder* (New York: Oxford University Press, 2010), 49-77.

2. For a convenient translation of the Babylonian myth of creation, see Stephanie Dalley, *Myths from Mesopotamia: Creation, the Flood, Gilgamesh, and Others,* World's Classics (Oxford: Oxford University Press, 1991), 228-77.

defeated by Babylon's imperial deity, Marduk, who according to Meso-potamian myth slew the gods of chaos and proclaimed himself lord of the universe. Marduk's calling card was "creation by conquest." Brutalized and humiliated, the survivors desperately needed hope and some semblance of dignity in the land of exile.

Enter Genesis 1. No clash of the Titans here. Only God, Israel's unri-valed deity. This God in Genesis creates not through conquest but by com-mand, by collaboration rather than through conflict. Lacking any hint of polemical nastiness, Genesis 1 served as a textual form of nonviolent re-sistance against imperial oppression and influence, whether Babylonian or Persian. Through its own account of cosmic creation, the exiled community sustained its identity amid the pressures of cultural assimilation, on the one hand, and national despair, on the other. With the edict of release issued in 538 B.C.E. by Babylon's conqueror, the Persian king Cyrus II, the op-portunity availed itself for the exiles to return and rebuild. In its historical context, Genesis 1 offers a cosmically hopeful vision for those ready to begin the great collaborative work of restoration, a monumental task of biblical proportions, a rebuilding program that does not require a native monarchy (forbidden under Persian rule) but instead affirms, as we shall see, the di-vinely endowed worth of every individual, made in "the image of God." In this text, the God of the primordial beginning proves to be the God of ever new beginnings. Genesis 1, it turns out, constructs a cosmic edifice of hope.

Primordial Soup

But first, back to the beginning, or at least to the beginning described in the first two verses. The curtain rises to reveal a dark, cosmic mishmash:

> When God began to create the heavens and the earth,[3] the earth was void and vacuum, and darkness was upon the surface of the deep while the breath of God hovered over the water's surface. (Gen. 1:1-2)

3. Contrary to the King James Version translation ("In the beginning God created the heavens and the earth"), the first verse in Gen. 1 is not a complete sentence in Hebrew. For discussion of the syntactical issues, see William P. Brown, *Structure, Role, and Ideology in the Hebrew and Greek Texts of Genesis 1:1–2:3,* Society of Biblical Literature Dissertation Series 132 (Atlanta: Scholars Press, 1993), 62-72; and, for an alternative proposal with similar outcome, Robert D. Holmstedt, "The Restrictive Syntax of Genesis i 1," *Vetus Testamentum* 58 (2008): 56-67.

This initial state is described as *tohu wabohu,* a wonderfully poetic phrase translated here as "void and vacuum."[4] The Hebrew, however, is more vivid. The phrase is an alliterative meshing of two Hebrew words whose semantic sense transcends its individual components, as in "topsy-turvy," "vice versa," "mishmash," "hodgepodge," "mingle-mangle." It designates, in other words, a farrago — a messy, confused mixture or conglomeration.[5] Such was the "soupy" state of the universe in the beginning, according to the ancient cosmologist of Genesis. One could call it chaos, but not in any mythically threatening sense. This "chaos" is no enemy of God. Darkness, water, and emptiness together do not make a monster. But neither do they constitute mere nothingness *(nihil).* To find God creating something from nothing *(creatio ex nihilo),* one must look elsewhere in later tradition (e.g., 2 Macc. 7:28). Genesis 1, rather, depicts *creatio ex chao,* creation out of a soupy mishmash, a watery, roiling, empty waste of a state. Genesis 1:2 describes a state of dynamic disorder poised for the in-breaking of order. With God's breath suspended over the dark, turbid waters, the stage is now set for a dramatically creative act, a cosmic blast of light.

The Legacy and Levity of Light

"Let light be!" As God's first words (only two in Hebrew) shatter the cosmic silence, so God's first act splits the primordial darkness. This command marks God's exhalation of *ruach,* which can be translated "breath," "wind," or "spirit." "Breath," I'm convinced, is the best choice in 1:2, from the simple fact that, by analogy, exhaling is essential for speaking, and God does plenty of speaking in Genesis 1. (Try speaking while inhaling.) God's breath "hovering"[6] over the watery darkness, pregnant with potential, is God's breath waiting to be released. And with breath released, so light is unleashed.[7] God in Genesis 1 "exhales," as it were, ten times in speech to bring about creation. God breathes out at every step in the process, ini-

---

4. See Mark S. Smith, *The Priestly Vision of Genesis 1* (Minneapolis: Fortress, 2010), 50-51.

5. The French expression *le tohu-bohu,* meaning "hubbub," is a Hebrew loanword that captures well the biblical sense.

6. For comparable use of the verb *rhp,* see Deut. 32:11, in which the mother eagle or vulture is depicted "hovering" over her brood, suggesting a more intimate relationship between God and the dark waters than is usually assumed.

7. See the discussion of light's unique "creation" in Smith, *Priestly Vision,* 71-79.

tiating creation through uttered word, and the result is a cosmos replete with variety, structure, and the greatest wonder of all: life!

So why is light the first act of creation? The text does not say. Clearly, light is intimately associated with God. This primordial light bears the radiance of the divine. But there may be another side to light shining in the darkness, hinted at by a winsome paraphrase of the first three verses of Genesis:

> Now when the Almighty was first down with his program, He made the heavens and the earth. The earth was a fashion misfit, being so uncool and dark, but the Spirit of the Almighty came down real tough, so that He simply said, "Lighten up!" And that light was right on time. And the Almighty liked what He saw and let the light hang out a while before it was dark again.[8]

It is fun to imagine God's first words infusing the gloomy universe with a sense of levity. Did God find dark chaos "so uncool" because, among other things, it was so seriously dull? Was the unleashing of light God's way of livening up the cosmos, of instilling playfulness into the lugubrious mix? Is levity part of light's cosmic legacy? Something to wonder about.

In any case, it is by no means coincidental that light was God's first act of creation. As any astrophysicist will tell you, light is "the most obvious and fundamental medium of our connection to the universe."[9] According to Genesis 1, light also has to do with God's connection to creation. As a parallel account of creation, Psalm 104 refers to light as God's own clothing (104:1-2). Light evidently bears an affinity to the divine. In Genesis 1, it is under the gleam of divine light that everything else is created, "seen," and declared good, including the celestial bodies on the fourth day. For Genesis, the light of the first day is not reducible to the light emitted by the sun, moon, and constellations. They are derived lights. By God's own light, God "sees" everything created and declares it all "very good" (1:31). Such light is the medium of divine perception.[10] In the pronouncement

---

8. P. K. McCary, *Black Bible Chronicles*, vol. 1: *From Genesis to the Promised Land* (New York: African American Family, 1993), 2. My thanks to Michael Morgan for bringing this "translation" to my attention.

9. Lee Smolin, *The Life of the Cosmos* (London: Phoenix, 1997), 27.

10. But compare the psalmist's observation: "Even darkness is not dark to you; the night is as bright as day, for darkness is as light to you" (Ps. 139:12). Divine perception is not equivalent to human perception.

"let light be," in the release of divine breath, God's eyes are opened, as it were, and creation commences.

Light, moreover, constitutes a cosmic domain in Genesis 1, the very first domain. With the creation of light, and its subsequent separation from the darkness (1:4), space itself is defined. So also time: evening and morning mark the first day (1:5), and every subsequent day as well. By virtue of their common origin in Genesis (and in astrophysics), space and time are fundamentally related. They are the foundational constituents of physical reality, hence their priority in cosmic history, whether in the Big Bang of modern cosmology or in the Big Flash of Genesis 1. Everything thereafter, from lilies to Leviathan, is a matter of light's legacy.

The Genesis Code

Speaking of "big," the big picture conjured in Genesis 1 is itself a marvel, and it can be seen only by stepping back and viewing the text's overall structure. It is, I submit, the "secret" message of Genesis 1, a secret at least to most modern readers, and it is such a jaw-dropping revelation that I call it the "Genesis Code," not to be confused with *The Da Vinci Code* by Dan Brown (no relation), but just as sensational in my opinion. Deciphering this code is not some irrelevant detail to our discussion; it is the key to understanding Genesis 1 as a whole. The secret lies in pattern recognition.[11]

In the first three days of creation, certain cosmic domains are established: first light, then the sky, the waters, and the land. In the second set of three days, each domain becomes populated with its own members: lights, marine life, aviary life, and land animals, including human beings. In the course of creation a remarkable symmetry unfolds, outlined in the diagram on page 21. According to their thematic correspondences, the first six days of creation form two parallel columns. Their chronological ordering gives rise to a thematic symmetry. Days 1-3 delineate the cosmic domains, which are then populated by various entities or agencies that fit these domains (days 4-6). Read vertically, the two columns address the two abject conditions of lack described in 1:2, formlessness and empti-

11. For further detail, see Brown, *Seven Pillars of Creation,* 38-41; and S. Dean McBride Jr., "Divine Protocol: Genesis 1:1–2:3 as Prologue to the Pentateuch," in *God Who Creates: Essays in Honor of W. Sibley Towner,* ed. William P. Brown and S. Dean McBride Jr. (Grand Rapids: Eerdmans, 2000), 3-41 at 12-15.

"Day 0" void and vacuum (1:2)	
Day 1 (1:3-5) light	**Day 4** (1:14-19) lights
Day 2 (1:6-8) sky waters below	**Day 5** (1:20-23) aviary life marine life
Day 3 (1:9-13) land vegetation	**Day 6** (1:24-31) land animals humans food
Day 7 (2:1-3) creation completed	

ness. The left column (days 1-3) recounts the *form*-ation of creation, while the right hand column (days 4-6) describes creation being *filled*. Day 3 serves as the link by depicting the emergence of land: with vegetation the earth is now a fructified land, providing the means for sustaining life. Days 4-6 report the filling of the empty domains with their respective inhabitants, from the celestial spheres, which "rule" both day and night, to human beings, who exercise "dominion." Astral bodies and human bodies bear a functional correspondence: both are given the task of ruling. With the stars set in the heavens and the various forms of life filling the sky, land, and sea, creation proceeds from emptiness to fullness in the right hand column, just as it had proceeded from formlessness to form-fullness in the left hand column.

What, then, about the seventh day? Having no corresponding partner, this day is unique. With its presence, the six-day symmetry of the Genesis account is broken. Ask any particle physicist, and she will tell you that it is in the breaking of symmetry that everything interesting emerges. So also in Genesis 1: this distinctly oddball day, by breaking the symmetry of the six-day structure, imbues it with near revelatory significance, as we shall see. First to note is that this seventh day establishes a subtle *vertical* correspondence to creation's initial condition, as described in 1:2, which one could call, paradoxically, "day 0," the "day" before time. Together these two "days" exhibit a hidden correlation, the static, timeless "day" of non-creation and the "theostatic" seventh day. Both lack the temporal formula, "evening came and then morning." The final day is a day suspended above temporal regularities, a day that transcends time even as "day 0" precedes time. Yet these two "days" could not be more different: "day 0" points to creation unformed and empty (1:2); day 7 marks creation fully formed and filled (2:1). It is the only day declared "holy" by God. The seventh day, moreover, turns out to be the capstone for the entire structure, for without it the overall pattern would lose a peculiar distinction that remains largely hidden to modern readers. Therein lies the "Genesis Code."

To ancient readers of Genesis, the "code" needed no deciphering; they would have recognized the pattern exhibited in Genesis 1, namely a threefold structure representing the architecture of a typical temple.[12] Solomon's temple as described in 1 Kings 6, for example, consists of three spatial parts: an outer vestibule or portico, the nave or main room, and the innermost sanctum located at the far back of the temple, the holy of holies (Hebrew *debir*), which only the high priest could enter once a year:

Portico
Nave
Holy of Holies

This threefold arrangement of sacred space corresponds precisely to the way in which the various days of creation are distributed both chronologically and thematically. The first six days, by virtue of their correspondence, demarcate the architectural boundaries of sacred space. The last day, given its uniqueness, is lodged in the most holy space:

12. Typical, that is, of the Syro-Palestinian region. For architectural details, see Michael B. Hundley, *Gods in Dwellings: Temples and Divine Presence in the Ancient Near East*, Writings from the Ancient World Supplement Series 3 (Atlanta: Society of Biblical Literature, 2013), 105-14.

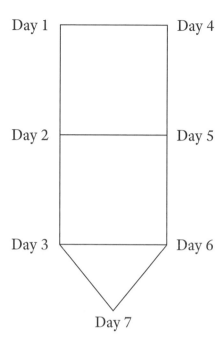

What, then, is the message behind the Genesis Code? It is this: the cosmos is cast in the image of the temple! The universe, according to Genesis 1, is God's cosmic sanctuary. Creation's "entrance," as it were, is established by days 1 and 4, featuring the creation of light and lights. Not coincidentally, the Solomonic temple in Jerusalem, like many temples of its time and vicinity, faced eastward toward the rising sun, whose rays illuminated the temple's gilded furnishings every morning (on clear days). On the other end chronologically and spatially, the holy seventh day marks God's completion of creation, God's "rest," which corresponds to the holy sanctum, where God is said to reside in "thick darkness" (1 Kings 8:12).[13] Rest and residence, in other words, find their holy correspondence in creation and temple. The temple, thus, is truly a microcosmos; the universe, in turn, is a macrotemple. Creation is God's first temple.

In sum, the chronological framework of Genesis 1 reflects the spatial framework of the temple. In the seven days of creation lies the threefold

13. Reference to "thick darkness" in the Holy of Holies in the temple, similar to the description of precreation in Gen. 1:2, preserves God's transcendence beyond time and space. God began to create in the dark, so God remains in the dark. (For images of light and darkness with respect to God, see chapter 4.)

structure of sacred space. In Genesis, time and space are wedded together in God's cosmic sanctuary. Einstein would be proud. So would Rachel Carson. The central message of Genesis is that all of creation, from every living thing made "according to its kind" to the celestial spheres regulating the seasons, has a place in God's holy temple, and Sabbath is creation's capstone. Respect for God's creation has no greater warrant than here; respect for creation is tantamount to reverence of God, the creator of all. Creation *is* God's holy sanctuary. The "sacred depths of nature" are truly sacred.[14]

Image of God

As for humanity's place in God's cosmic temple, the Genesis Code reveals something profoundly wondrous. Typically, a temple contained an image of its resident deity within its inner sanctum. In ancient Jerusalem, however, the physical representation of God was expressly forbidden, as stipulated in a certain commandment: "You shall not make for yourself an idol" (Exod. 20:4; Deut. 5:8). God was considered without discernible form and thus could not be represented (Deut. 4:12-18). According to biblical lore, the inner sanctum of the Jerusalem temple contained the "ark of the covenant" covered by the outstretched wings of two cherubim (1 Kings 6:23-28). The ark was regarded as both God's footstool and the container of the stone tablets of the Decalogue. Instead of a statue of God, the statutes of God were housed in the temple.

But Genesis 1 does something quite radical. Far from renouncing the language of divine image, Genesis 1 identifies the *imago Dei* with human beings, created on the sixth day:

> Then God said, "Let us make humanity in our image [*tselem*],
>   after our likeness [*demut*]. . . ."
> So God created the human being in his image,
>   in the image of God he created them;
>   male and female he created them. (1:26a, 27)

The creation of humanity is unique. Nowhere else in Genesis does God command the divine assembly to collaborate in creation, and nowhere

---

14. See Ursula Goodenough, *The Sacred Depths of Nature* (Oxford: Oxford University Press, 1998).

else is the term "image" used. Human beings alone bear a distinctly iconic relation to the divine. The Hebrew term for "image" *(tselem)* is elsewhere used primarily for idols, such as the statues of other deities. Beyond the Bible, ancient Near Eastern literature frequently refers to the king, be he Babylonian or Assyrian, as the exclusive "image" of the deity. Genesis, however, takes a more democratic approach: all human beings take on the royal status of near divinity. While God lacks a blatantly anthropomorphic profile in Genesis 1 (at least compared to Gen. 2–3), human beings assume a distinctively "theomorphic," or godlike, form. Made in God's image, human beings reflect and refract God's presence in the world. According to Genesis, the only appropriate "image of God" is one made of flesh, of blood, bone, and brain, not wood, gold, or plastic. And one need not wield a royal scepter to qualify. A pen or pencil will do just fine.

But does this mean that these walking, talking theophanies have license to do whatever they want? When it comes to celebrating humanity's dominion over creation, the next two verses are critical:

> God said, "I hereby give to you every seed-bearing plant on the face of all the earth, and every tree with seed in its fruit. They shall be yours for food. And to every animal of the earth, and to every bird of the air, and to everything that creeps on the earth, everything that has the breath of life, I give every green plant for food." And it was so. (Gen. 1:29-30)

God gives all the edible plants to *both* humans and animals. (Nothing, by the way, is said about meat.) We humans, thus, are not to hoard the means of sustenance but to ensure that all life has sufficient resources to thrive together. Genesis fully acknowledges that the human animal shares the planet with other animals, and this planet is meant to host them all. While *Homo sapiens* is no plague animal, an invasive species that wreaks havoc on the rest of life because it lacks natural predators, the high and mighty human is by no means the "end all" of life on the earth. Genesis acknowledges the inherent goodness of life's diversity, from swarming schools of fish to the murmurations of starlings, from "sea monsters" to hummingbirds, each created "according to its kind." God has created a richly biogenic planet, one that accommodates a multitude of species, each having its niche in the geological and climatic diversity of creation, each finding a place (or nook or cranny) in God's cosmic temple.

"We are as gods and might as well get good at it," pronounced Stewart Brand in the first edition of the *Whole Earth Catalog* in 1968. He has recently revised his motto: "We are as gods, and we have to get good at it."[15] Although the author of Genesis would put it differently ("We are God's images"), Brand has captured well the high calling of humanity in Genesis. The human species is the most powerful species on earth, able to wield dominion over all creation, and that in itself is a thing of wonder. But we also have it within us to be the most responsible species on earth, and to exercise that would be an even greater wonder.

The Collaborative God

Humanity's God-given dominion takes its cue from the kind of God human beings, made in God's image, are made to reflect. Take, for example, Genesis 1:11-12:

> Then God said, "Let the earth sprout vegetation: plants bearing seed and fruit trees of every kind on earth that bear fruit with seed in it." And it was so. The earth brought forth vegetation: plants bearing seed of every kind and trees of every kind bearing fruit with seed in it.

God does *not* say, "Let there be vegetation," as in the singular case of light (1:3). Instead, God enlists the earth to create life, specifically plant life. Later, the earth is commanded to bring forth animal life (1:24). The earth itself is acknowledged, by God no less, as a creative and sustaining power, a truly collaborative agent. So also the waters in 1:20-21:

> Then God said, "Let the waters produce swarms of living creatures." . . . So God created the great sea monsters and every living creature that moves, of which the waters produced swarms, according to their kinds. . . . And God saw that it was good.

The waters, too, are acknowledged as bearers of life. Together God and the waters bring forth marine life. When it comes to creating life, God works collaboratively. Far from being inert, the earth and the waters are themselves reckoned as creative agents: God works *with* them, not against

15. Stewart Brand, *Whole Earth Discipline: An Ecopragmatist Manifesto* (New York: Viking, 2009), 20.

them. The same goes for God's final act: humanity. God says, "Let us make humankind in our image" (1:26). Humanity itself is the product of collaborative work. And whom did God enlist this time? Jewish tradition claims Wisdom; Christian tradition claims the Trinity (the Son and the Spirit with the Father). Ecologists might claim the earth and the waters, which have already been creating at God's behest. The ancient author may have had the divine assembly in mind, that is, the "sons of God" or heavenly beings/angels (Job 1–2). Perhaps all of the above, the panoply of heaven and earth taking part in this culminating act of creation. One can only wonder.

In any event, the grand and glorious result is creation's "goodness." "Good," repeated seven times in Genesis 1, acknowledges creation's ordered integrity and intrinsic value. "Good" affirms creation's sustainability, its proclivity for fecundity. The world deemed "good" by God is creation set toward the furtherance of life: plants and fruit trees regenerate through their seeds; vegetation sustains all land animals, including humans; and all animals reproduce. Robust, resilient, evolving life is definitive of creation's "goodness." Through seeds, sex, and brains, God has created a creating world.

Finally, God's last act of creation is not one lone human being standing at the apex of creation but a collective, fully gendered humanity, male and female, working with God in creation. Women and men *together* embody God's image. It is our gendered diversity, so claims the ancient writer, that reflects God. So also our ethnic and cultural diversities, so we might infer. I wonder, then, whether the *imago Dei* is more than a mirror reflecting some singular aspect of the divine focused on a single faculty of the human, such as rationality, and more like a prism refracting divine light into the vast spectrum of humanity's differences and distinctions, its races and ethnicities — black, brown, gold, red, yellow, white — infinite shades of various colors and cultures, as well as faculties and gifts, all conveying the manifold, interrelated character of God in the world. Such would be the legacy of light.

Wondering about the Beginning

There is much wonder to behold in Genesis 1. God for one: the divine collaborator at work enlisting the elements of creation to create life according to all its various "kinds." Creation for another: a finely tuned, life-hosting world cast as God's living temple generously endowed with the natural capacities to bear and sustain life in all its diversity. And as for human beings, we are nothing less than God's walking, talking theophanies on earth. With humanity blessed with such high status, the stakes are also high for all life on earth.

As there is much wonder to behold in Genesis, there is also much to wonder about in the text. This grand creation account gives one pause to ponder why there is a world at all. "In the beginning God created the heavens and the earth" (King James Version); "in the beginning when God created" (New Revised Standard Version); "when God began to create" (New Jewish Publication Society Translation). Regardless of how one translates the first verse and all that follows, nowhere do we find a specific reason as to why God created in the first place, why there is something rather than nothing, light rather than darkness, structure rather than *tohu,* life rather than emptiness. Did God suffer an acute case of loneliness? Was God in dire need of relationship? Does God need a world to be God? The text is silent. It certainly admits of no compulsion, let alone a reason on God's part. God simply created. Period. And the reader is left in the throes of ontological wonder.

Stepping beyond the text, I wonder what might have inspired God to create in the first place. Perhaps God fashioned a world simply out of loving curiosity with only a rough sketch in mind, no detailed blueprint, to see what would happen. God created to see, for instance, what kinds of plants would sprout out of the soil. God created to behold the manifold variety of life the waters and the earth would produce. God might have created simply for the love of creating, "just because," in hope that a relationship would emerge in whatever form that might take. I suspect that behind the emotional reserve of Genesis 1 lies a passion overflowing from God's own heart, the kind of inspiration that artists feel when starting a new project without having a fixed image of how their work will turn out, always a risky but thrilling venture. Such is the artist's way. God's creation, in other words, emerged from that improvisational convergence of possibility and purpose, of freedom and direction, of order and chaos. It is no coincidence that God's cosmic masterpiece embodies both.

The artist's satisfaction at certain steps in the process, and particularly at the work's completion, is an ineffable joy, a Sabbath joy. Perhaps a booming "yes!" accompanied every pronouncement of "good," and a raucous "wow!" erupted at the climactic "very good," marking creation's completion. But the biblical author was too reserved to convey any of that. And what about the seventh day? I doubt that God's "rest" was out of fatigue.

Instead, I imagine God "resting" out of desire, a holy desire, to enjoy the wonder of it all. That first Sabbath day, God's concluding "act," provided space and time for God to ponder and enjoy, to wonder and delight, and it began with God letting go so that creation could go on, taking on a life of its own. It is the only day that is blessed by God; it is the only day in which God does nothing. The holy Sabbath was made for God and for creation, a blessing for its benefit, a blessing for our benefit (cf. Mark 2:27-28). Such is the blessing of cessation. Such is the blessing of contemplative wonder.

From the cosmic to the quantum, creation is the original *acte gratuit.* The greatest mystery may not be that there is a God but that there is a world.[16] Knowing that makes my little, less than cosmic world a bit more wondrous too.

16. See Karl Barth, *Dogmatics in Outline,* trans. G. T. Thomson (London: SCM, 1959), 54.

29

2. *Grounded Wonder*

GENESIS 2:4B–3:24

> Then the LORD God formed the groundling from the dust of
> the ground.
>
> *Genesis 2:7*

The story of Adam and Eve in the garden presents a different kind of creation, one that is less cosmological and more anthropological. Genesis
2:4b–3:24 (henceforth Genesis 2–3) rewinds the tape of creation and re-
plays it from a very different angle and with a very different outcome.
Whereas Genesis 1 presents a cosmic panorama with everything set in its
proper place, Genesis 2–3 gives us a messy family drama. It is a deceptively
simple tale, but one that is rich with ambiguity and generative of searching
questions. Stripped of the veneer that has accumulated on its surface over
centuries of strained interpretation, mostly Christian, the story shimmers
with irony and paradox. Like Genesis 1, this account of creation is a story
to marvel over and to wonder about. But the kind of wonder Genesis 2–3
evokes is less majestic and more intimate and painful, a down-to-earth
kind of wonder. It is, after all, a garden story, a drama full of dirt.

The Garden as History

It might be good at the outset to share how I read the garden story before
exploring what I find particularly wondrous about it. How to read Genesis

2–3 continues to be a contentious issue among readers today. Is the story historical? Was there an actual Adam, along with an Eve and a talking snake, not to mention an oasis paradise from which they were expelled? Was there a time in which perfect harmony existed between humans and animals, after which everything fell into tragic conflict and needless suffering because of a human couple's disobedience? Posed this way, I would have to say, No. I do not take the story so literally. Humans were not created first and then the animals.[1] There was never a time on earth in which nature existed in perfect harmony. Predation, suffering, and death have always been operative on this planet since the beginning of life.

Nevertheless, I would claim that Genesis 2–3 *is* historical, and in a very fundamental sense. It illuminates a dynamic of human history that repeats itself time and again, namely, our tendency to grasp for power in ways that result in tragedy. More broadly, the story of Adam and Eve vividly illustrates a painful part of human development, the emergence of consciousness and conscience. While the garden story is not itself historical in any literal sense, it is paradigmatic of human history. The story provides a framework to account for the aspirations and tragedies of humanity's evolving identity in the world, and for me that makes the story all the more profound and, yes, wondrous. Its wonder comes not from any inner historicity but from its powerful framing of a plot that spins itself in countless variations, politically, economically, interpersonally, psychologically, ecologically.

The Garden as Story

So back to the plot and its various characters. God for one: if God is king of the cosmos in Genesis 1, then God is king of the compost in Genesis 2. In Genesis 2, God wields a garden spade instead of a royal scepter. The God from on high becomes the God on the ground, a down-and-dirty deity. This is clear from the very beginning: instead of the dark waters of cosmic "chaos" swirling around in dynamic disorder in Genesis 1 (1:2), Genesis 2 begins with a barren stretch of land, a land of lack: no rain, no plants, no tiller (2:5), as if to say simply: "In the beginning . . . dirt." But

---

1. See my more detailed presentation of the story in conversation with science in William P. Brown, *The Seven Pillars of Creation: The Bible, Science, and the Ecology of Wonder* (New York: Oxford University Press, 2010), 92-114.

as any gardener knows, dirt is deceptive. Dirt (or soil) bears the hidden potential for growth, depending on its composition. The soil in Genesis 2 is no doubt fertile, for it provides the groundwork of all creation, including human creation.

Nevertheless, in the beginning is a land of lack. But this is quickly remedied: a subterranean stream rises to the surface to moisten the soil, and God, like a potter, fashions a human being *(adam)* from dirt and then, as a gardener, plants a garden. God goes all natural here. The purpose in all this? To cultivate community, perhaps simply to enjoy fellowship in this garden of plenty and delight.[2] Regardless, the God we meet in the garden is no outsider making a grand entrance to the blaring of trumpets. God is simply there working the soil, walking around, and enjoying the evening breeze with others.

The Ground and the Groundling: A World-Play

To sustain the garden, God creates a human being, or *adam* in Hebrew, otherwise known as "Adam" but without the proper name:

> The LORD God formed the *adam* from the dust of the ground [*adamah*] and breathed into "his" nostrils the breath of life; and the *adam* became a living being. (2:7)

Here, the *adam* is made not in the *imago Dei,* as Genesis 1 has it, but in the *imago terrae,* in the image of the ground, of earth. Humanity here is rooted in the soil. We are children of the earth, the ancient storyteller tells us, as much as we are children of God, made in God's image, as Genesis 1 claims. As is well known to readers of Hebrew, humanity's created identity in Genesis 2 is established by a remarkable wordplay: the *adam* is fashioned from the "dust of the *adamah.*" The word for "ground" *(adamah)* in Hebrew looks like a feminine form of *adam,* and therein lies the first significant gender distinction in the story: "ground" (grammatically feminine in Hebrew) and "human" (grammatically masculine in Hebrew). The masculine is created from the feminine, both sharing common ground. The *adam* is

---

2. Or as John Wierwille, pastor elder of Berea Mennonite Church in Atlanta and director of Oakleaf Mennonite Farm, puts it: "God simply wanted to hang out in a garden with a couple of naked vegetarians" (personal communication).

fashioned from the *adamah,* the human from the fertile *humus,*[3] a human "soul" from the soil.[4] Soil, the ancient tale contends, is integral to humanity's makeup. This human creature, not yet distinctly male (see below), is inseparably tied to the ground from which "he" came.

But there is another step in the *adam's* genesis that reveals God's intimate and "natural" nature. The *adam* becomes a "living being" only after receiving the "breath of life" from God. How does that happen? Quite differently from the way Michelangelo famously portrayed Adam's creation on the ceiling of the Sistine Chapel. There we see two outstretched fingers millimeters apart: Adam's finger raised upward toward God and God's finger stretched down to meet Adam's. If Michelangelo had actually painted the episode more in keeping with the biblical story, the result would have looked shockingly different: not finger to finger but mouth to nose (2:7). In Genesis 2 God performs something akin to CPR, or more accurately CPS: cardiopulmonary "suscitation." Call it the divine kiss. This God is a hands-on deity — mouth too.

With this groundling transplanted in the garden, the narrative shifts abruptly to describing Eden's water system (2:10-14). Out of Eden flow four rivers to water the whole world: the Pishon, the Gihon, the Tigris, and the Euphrates. The list moves from the unknown to the known. The last two rivers are geographically identifiable. Indeed, the land of Mesopotamia ("Between Rivers") refers to the region bounded by the Tigris and the Euphrates. The first two rivers, however, extend to unknown lands laden with precious stones. These rivers are clearly more mythic in nature. Together, they provide a clue to Eden's "location." They place the garden on the cognitive horizon between myth and reality. In fact, the name "Eden" has to do more with condition than with geography; the word designates a state of delight and plenty *('dn),* the sheer opposite of lack and deprivation (cf. Gen. 18:12; Ps. 36:8; Neh. 9:25; Jer. 31:12; 51:34; Ezek. 36:35; Joel 2:3). But Eden is no pristine paradise of leisure, for it requires tending. The *adam* must "serve" and "preserve" the rich soil of this edible landscape (2:15). The *adam* is tied to the *adamah* in service as the *adamah* yields to the *adam* its productivity, a symbiosis made in heaven . . . on earth!

---

3. The etymological connection endures even in English (with a little help from Latin).

4. So in conjunction with the King James Version, which translates the end of Gen. 2:7 as "living soul." But this is not the best translation: "living being" (New Revised Standard Version) is a better one for the Hebrew *nephesh hayyah.* For discussion, see Brown, *Seven Pillars of Creation,* 109-10.

Unlike other ancient creation accounts outside the Bible, human beings in Genesis 2 are not created to perform menial labor for the gods, who themselves loathe such toil. God evidently enjoys grubbing about in the soil, and the *adam* is there to preserve the garden that nourishes him. The garden exists for the groundling and the groundling for the garden. The *adam* is given wide-ranging freedom with only one specific restriction: he is granted access to "every tree of the garden" except one, the "tree of the knowledge of good and bad" (2:16-17). The capacity for autonomous judgment, along with the freedom to act on it, is not (yet) the groundling's prerogative.

While not everything in the garden is for the groundling's use, God does seem to have the *adam's* best interests at heart. For the first time in Genesis, God declares creation "not good."[5] While providing sufficient support for the *adam's* physical welfare, the garden is deemed deficient for the groundling's social well-being. Lacking a companion, the groundling in the garden remains in solitary confinement. As remedy, God creates a host of animals of various species, also "out of the ground," and brings them to the *adam*. The narrative acknowledges that humans and all other animals share the same substance. From God's perspective they all share common ground. But not so, as it turns out, from the *adam's* perspective. By naming the animals, the primal human configures a differentiated community, but a community that lacks an equal partner, literally "a corresponding helper" (2:18). And so the search is on for a full partner in service to the garden and a companion equal to the *adam*. Although sharing a measure of identity with the animals, the *adam* does not recognize any one of them as a potential match and mate; the groundling sees nothing of "his" own flesh and bone among the other animals (2:23). God's initial experiment has failed, but the results are by no means discarded. The animals are left in the garden to thrive along with the *adam*, groundlings all of them.

The Woman and the Man: Another World-Play

God proceeds to Plan B, a more invasive procedure. Only in this way can an equal partner be created, a partner fashioned from the *adam's* own flesh and bone, comparable to the "groundling" fashioned from the "ground."

---

5. Compare God's declaration of "good" in Gen. 1:4, 10, 12, 18, 21, 25, 31.

Although deemed a "helper" *(ezer),*[6] the woman is no subordinate being; she is the man's perfect counterpart. This new creation requires the
extraction of a part of the *adam,* namely his "side" (Hebrew *tsela*).[7] This
surgical procedure is no one-way derivation, however, for it is from the
creation of the woman *(ishshah)* that the *adam* finally becomes a "man"
(ish). The first time that the *adam* is referred to as a "man" in the Hebrew
is in Genesis 2:23. Only then is the *adam* truly a "he," the direct result of
the woman's creation. God's surgical procedure, in other words, marks
the mutual engendering of humanity. With the creation of the woman,
humanity is now "genderly" separated. Call it the splitting of the *adam.*

What a paradoxical wonder! Through the act of surgical *removal,*
one would expect the *adam* to be neutered. Quite the contrary. It is precisely in his physical loss that the *adam* gains his male identity, along with
a partner. The groundling receives his manhood in relation to the woman
who now stands facing him. The newly fashioned woman bears a direct
physical correspondence to this newly fashioned man, and his response is
one of utter (and uttered) jubilation. His cry of joy acknowledges their fully
shared identity: "This finally is bone of my bones and flesh of my flesh; this
one shall be called Woman, for out of Man this one was taken" (Gen. 2:23).
Remarkably, no mention is made of their sexual differentiation. The man's
jubilation focuses on what they share in common: bone and flesh. Their
affinity, however, extends beyond biology.[8] The woman and the man find
themselves to be made in the image of each other, physically, socially, and
covenantally.[9] They are family. Having been fashioned in the *imago terrae,*
the adam discovers *him*self to be fashioned also in the woman's image,
and the woman in the man's. Together, they form a familial partnership of
correspondence, enjoying mutual companionship and fruitful service in
the garden of plenty.

With the creation of the woman, the man now bears a complete identity: he remains kin to the ground in his humanity as he has become kin

6. Beyond Gen. 2, the term *ezer* most often refers to God or divine aid (e.g., Exod.
18:4; Deut. 33:7, 26, 29; Ps. 33:20; 70:6; 115:9-11; 146:4) and, thus, need not suggest subordi-
nation. At the end of Gen. 2:18, the preposition *neged* in the composite phrase *kenegdo* literally means "in front of" or "opposite of," here in the sense of correspondence or counterpart.

7. Not "rib." For the same term elsewhere, see, e.g., Exod. 25:12, 14; 2 Sam. 16:13.

8. See, e.g., Laban's acknowledgement of Jacob in Gen. 29:14, as well as similar ex-
amples of this expression in Judges 9:2 and 2 Sam. 5:1.

9. See Walter Brueggemann, "Of the Same Flesh and Bone (Gen 2,23a)," *Catholic
Biblical Quarterly* 32 (1970): 532-42.

to the woman in his gendered identity. As the *adamah* is receptive to the *adam*'s labors, the *adam* receives the fruits of the *adamah*. The man and the woman, in turn, are receptive to each other. The *adam*'s service to the garden is rooted in his mutual partnership with the ground. Marriage, according to the additional note in 2:24, hangs on mutual intimacy and partnership as well (without mention of children, I might add). In other words, companionship pure and simple. And in such companionship, there is neither fear nor shame, even before God. These are the "lacks" that are meant to endure. But, alas, they do not.

Becoming Human

A new scene opens in Genesis 3 with an entirely new character. The serpent is no garden-variety animal, but neither is it by any measure satanic, contrary to the weight of Christian tradition. The snake distinguishes itself only by its "craftiness" *(arum)*[10] in its ability to tailor truth, as we shall see. Dietrich Bonhoeffer observed that the serpent initiates the first conversation about God in the Bible,[11] which would qualify it as the Bible's first theologian. By engaging the woman in dialogue about God's intentions, the serpent aims to conjure a perceived lack in the couple's life together, one that prompts them to take matters into their own hands. The serpent draws the woman into conversation with a patently absurd claim,[12] which, if true, would have resulted in the couple's starvation. Correcting the serpent's feigned nonsense, the woman responds by faithfully recalling God's prohibition given to the *adam* in 2:17, recasting it even more stringently: not only are they to avoid eating from the fruit tree growing in the middle of the garden, they are not even to touch it (3:4). But the serpent is interested not in the precise formulation of God's prohibition but in its consequences. The sly creature arouses doubt by claiming that divine wisdom and power will follow, not punishment. They will "not die," the serpent contends; instead their eyes "will open," and they will assume divine status (3:4-5).

Prompted by the serpent's alleged clarification, the woman considers the tree. She lingers in awe over it. She sees that the tree is a "delight to the

10. The term for crafty or clever can have positive connotations in Proverbs (e.g., 13:16; 14:8; 22:3). It is also a wordplay on the word "naked" *(arom)* in Gen. 2:25.

11. Dietrich Bonhoeffer, *Creation and Fall: A Theological Interpretation of Genesis 1–3; Temptation*, trans. John C. Fletcher (London: SCM, 1959), 69.

12. The Hebrew lacks a question mark.

eyes" and its fruit delectable and desirable for wisdom (3:6). Such wisdom, the serpent promises, will result in self-enhancement of the highest order, an apotheosis no less. Yes, this tree, the tree of wisdom, of "the knowledge of good and bad," is a source of wonder, an irresistible object of desire.[13]

Yes, it is the woman who partakes, but she does so with the full complicity of her partner, "who was with her" (3:6b).[14] This all important but overlooked phrase is conveyed by only one word in Hebrew, a suffixed preposition *(immah)*. With it, the narrator makes clear that the woman does not act alone, even though the focus is on her initiative and on the attraction the tree holds for her. Was the woman deceived by, controlled by, or possessed by the serpent? Contrary to the weight of early Jewish and Christian interpretation, much of it influenced by the Greek myth of Pandora's Box,[15] the answer given by the narrator is a resounding "No!" The woman retains her agency; she comes to her own decision freely in light of the serpent's interpretation. It is especially significant that the narrator lingers over the woman's lingering over the tree. The tree itself is a wonder, and she is captivated by it (3:6a). Rather than being possessed by the serpent, the woman is tempted by the tree itself and makes her own judgment in light of its desirability. Who, indeed, would *not* want to partake of divine wisdom?

But the results, to put it mildly, prove disappointing. The couple's eyes are opened, just as the serpent said they would (3:5, 7). Anticipation builds as they are awakened to the seeming wonder of their new, divinely enhanced identity. But disaster occurs instead, the consequence, one might say, of trying to install a divine operating software system into animal-based hardware.[16] The system crashes, but not completely. Their eyes are opened wide enough only to recognize their naked vulnerability and feel shame. The desired trappings of divinity — power and immortal-

---

13. On the relationship between the tree and the woman's desire, see Carol A. Newsom, "Genesis 2–3 and *1 Enoch* 6–16: Two Myths of Origin and Their Ethical Implications," in *Shaking Heaven and Earth: Essays in Honor of Walter Brueggemann and Charles B. Cousar,* ed. Christine Roy Yoder et al. (Louisville: Westminster John Knox, 2005), 7-22 at 11-12.

14. The phrase is curiously (and shamefully) omitted in the Revised Standard Version and in several other translations. For a survey with accompanying analysis, see Julie Faith Parker, "Blaming Eve Alone: Translation, Omission, and Implications of '*mh* in Genesis 3:6b," *Journal of Biblical Literature* 132 (2013): 729-47.

15. See William E. Phipps, "Eve and Pandora Contrasted," *Theology Today* 45 (1988): 34-48.

16. Thanks to Carol Newsom for putting it this way.

ity — did not come, as expected. The irony of the outcome is heightened when God later states that eating from the "tree of knowledge" did, in fact, bring the couple a step closer to divinity: "The man has become like one of us, knowing good and bad" (3:22).

So the serpent was correct after all: their eyes were opened and they became "like God" (or "gods"; 3:5); moreover, they did not die upon eating the fruit. But the serpent did not tell the whole story: naked vulnerability, with accompanying shame, was also the result. Hence, the paradox: the attempted move toward divinity results in a step away from divinity yet a move toward becoming more human.[17] Knowledge, according to the narrative, does not necessarily translate into empowerment or self-enhancement. It can denigrate. Through their disobedience, they have become pale, vulnerable images of the divine. The lack outweighs the gain, and as such they have become fully human. The human being is the only animal that recognizes itself as naked, the only animal that requires clothing. Through the exercise of self-awareness or self-consciousness, humanity has distinguished itself from the animals even while sharing the same substance with them. Humanity is the "cross between ape and angel."[18]

The narrative continues with ever new twists. The couple's terrible awakening prompts them to hide from God, who casually strolls in the garden as apparently is God's custom (3:8). For the first time God's presence inspires fear and self-loathing. God demands an explanation. The man blames the woman ("whom you gave to be with me"),[19] who blames the serpent (it "misled me"). The blame game, however, does not come full circle, as one would expect, for God chooses not to interrogate the serpent. Had God done so, the serpent could have easily responded, "I only told the truth," thereby putting God on the defensive,[20] the God who created the tree, the serpent, and the humans in the first place. In God's refusal to interrogate the serpent, the series of unfortunate events now seems to be something of a setup.

Genesis 2–3 is a messy story, full of irony and ambiguity. With its dramatically evolving characters and open-ended, experimental plot, the

17. According to the logic of the narrative, partaking from the "tree of life" would have completed the couple's divinization, like installing new hardware (3:22).

18. Newsom, "Genesis 2–3," 20.

19. Note that the man is also blaming God (3:12).

20. See Danna N. Fewell and David M. Gunn, "Shifting the Blame: God in the Garden," in *Reading Bibles, Writing Bodies: Identity and the Book,* ed. Timothy K. Beal and David M. Gunn (London: Routledge, 1997), 16-33.

story builds to its suspenseful climax. The couple's partaking from the tree renders them self-transcendent, but not in any deified sense. They remain pitiful creatures, attaining enough consciousness to be *self*-conscious. They recognize themselves as vulnerable selves, exposed and deficient in relation to the divine. They realize, painfully so, that they are "naked," both frail and finite. Self-consciousness does not come easily, the story submits: it begins with a painful awareness of self-limitation. Whether in the garden or outside of it, becoming human is a hard row to hoe.

The garden story traces in one single sitting the tender, painful drama of growing up human. It is truth telling at its mythic best. The dramatic turning point that led to disobedience and self-consciousness had been building all along within the narrative. As the groundling was placed in the garden to "serve" and "preserve" (2:15), the first human was given a function, a job for which no moral assembly was required. At this point, human identity remained undeveloped. At the moment the prohibition was uttered, however, a new stage was reached: choice became a meaningful factor for the first time in the narrative. Disobedience was now possible. But the *adam* remained, as it were, a child faced with a parental command accompanied by the threat of punishment. The next stage of the couple's development came with the dilemma posed by both the snake's countertestimony, eliciting a measure of cognitive dissonance, and the tree's desirability for acquiring wisdom. The resulting disobedience emerged out of a conflictive mix of desire and dilemma. By partaking from the tree, the primal couple gained a level of self-consciousness, an awareness of their vulnerable condition and of their newly acquired ability to make decisions on their own. In so doing, they chose to grow up, with all its costs and complexities. Unwittingly, in their choice to become fully divine, they instead became fully human.

But a central question remains, a persistent wondering: Why would God forbid the primal couple from eating the fruit, from gaining self-consciousness and moral discernment, in the first place? Perhaps, as some have wondered, the timing was all wrong: the fruit had not ripened or the couple was not yet ready to receive it. But this seems too easy a solution. The answer instead may lie in the nature of the results, as the serpent had pointed out. In view of the consequences for the evolving characters, the fruit of consciousness and conscience (the story equates the two) *had* to be prohibited. There was no other choice. The fruit of knowledge was by necessity forbidden, for conscience, according to the logic of the text, could not have emerged otherwise. The narrative yields a profound psychological insight. Growth in conscience begins with facing the consequences of disobedience. To put it differently, conscience takes root in the soil of regret. It is the result of self-struggle and consequential choices. In its own evocative way, this short story navigates the painful complexities of becoming human. The garden story is more about growing than about falling.

Wondering in the Garden

This simple tale turns out to be richly provocative. It is, in other words, full of wonderings. Was the story a divine setup or an experiment? Was the serpent right? Did God expect the primal couple to disobey? Did Adam and Eve lose their immortality upon eating the fruit or did they lose their chance to become immortal once expelled? Did God know all along what was going to happen? What if the man and woman had conducted themselves differently after their disobedience? Here's where the story becomes particularly suggestive. How would God have reacted if, while strolling through the garden, the man and the woman had sheepishly joined God, rather than fleeing, and confessed their disobedience? If the couple had fully admitted their actions, would God have cast them out of the garden? What, in fact, was the real test: the temptation of the tree or the urge to blame and avoid responsibility? Failure on both counts: the couple chose to eat the forbidden fruit and they chose to blame, the man even blaming God (3:12). But what if they had taken responsibility for their actions? One can only wonder.

Yes, it all seems so sinful, but is there any significance to the word "sin" being absent in the story? It does not appear until the following chapter, when Cain considers murdering his brother, Abel. God articulates the challenge for Cain: "If you do what is right, will you not be accepted? And if you do not do what is right, sin is crouching at the door; its desire is for you, but you must master it" (4:7). Here, sin is cast as a crouching predator, poised to strike. The first mention of sin in the Bible is thus bound up with the impulse to commit violence, specifically fratricide, to which Cain tragically submits. How, then, is the couple's disobedience related to the violent unfolding of events in the following chapter? In what sense does the fig fall not far from the tree?

Speaking of trees, what about the *other* tree? Mentioned only in passing at the beginning of the story and reappearing only at its conclusion, the "tree of life" is itself something of an enigma. The text leaves open the possibility of whether the couple ate from it as they cared for and delighted in the garden, since only the "tree of knowledge" was expressly forbidden. So did they eat from it or not? I suspect they did not, for the tree of life was never an issue until the very end, on the occasion of the couple's expulsion. My guess is that as this tree was hidden from the reader's purview throughout most of the story, so it was also hidden from the couple's sight. The final scene has the couple barred from the garden to prevent them from returning and partaking from this particular tree to enable them to live "forever" (3:22). But as the story continues in Genesis 4, when the scene shifts from the garden to the inhospitable land, to the "dust of the ground," humanity as a species does not die but rather advances generation by generation.

God's blessing of life's continuation for human beings is tenderly indicated in 3:21. Although the couple is cursed and expelled, the man and the woman are by no means abandoned. After the curse, God clothes the couple, replacing their shriveled fig leaves, to prepare them for life outside the garden. Genesis 3 ends on expulsion *and* protection by God. In the very next chapter, Eve attributes the conception and successful birth of her son Cain to God's collaborative work (literally "with the LORD"; 4:1). Two chapters later, threatened with total extinction, life in all its diversity is preserved. It is as if God had plucked a branch from the tree of life and transplanted it *outside* the garden so as to preserve the human race within the rhythm of birth and death, the rhythm of womb and "dust" (3:19), of planting and reaping. (The word for "seed" in Hebrew can also mean "offspring.") The genealogical lists dispersed throughout the rest of Genesis and beyond (e.g., Gen. 10–11; 1 Chron. 1–9), all those "begats," attest to the flourishing branch of life. They attest to God's blessing of life rooted in Genesis 1. The human branch continues to survive as part of the much larger biological tree of life, firmly rooted and ever growing. The story of fecundity, the drama of dirt, continues, and the rest is history.

3. Covenantal Wonder

GENESIS 6–9

I have hung my bow in the clouds,
and it shall be a sign of the covenant between me
and the earth.

Genesis 9:13

Think of Noah and probably a rainbow comes to mind, one stretched over a wooden ship filled with cute, cuddly animals. Or, at the opposite extreme, one might think of an angry God bringing down a watery holocaust, drowning everyone in sight. The biblical story of Noah is neither a children's story nor a horror story. It is a re-creation story packed with a surprising twist that evokes wonder about who God is and how God becomes related to the world in a new way.

To understand the story of Noah, one must revisit the beginning of creation described in Genesis 1. There, creation began in primordial soup, a dark, watery mishmash (*tohu wabohu;* 1:2), from which God unleashed light from darkness and separated the waters above from the waters below. By establishing creation's infrastructure with its various cosmic domains, God set the stage for life, teeming in all its marvelous diversity: astral, aerial, marine, and terrestrial. Creation's goodness, referenced seven times in Genesis 1, points not only to its beauty but also to its sustainability. The plants of the earth bear seeds, making possible botanical succession. The command to "be fruitful and multiply and fill the earth" applies to human and nonhuman animals alike (1:22, 28). Seeds and sex, according to Genesis 1, make possible the earth's "plenishing." The story of Noah is all about the earth's replenishing.

Created in God's image, human beings have the additional and distinctive blessing of exercising "dominion" (1:26, 28). Such dominion involves care and wisdom, far from the kind of dominion that is harsh and cruel (cf. Ezek. 34:4). The God who created the world to be sustained is the God who commissions human beings to ensure creation's sustainability from generation to generation. Noah, it turns out, is the one who best carries out this commission, the one who most fully implements God's command to exercise sustainable dominion, fulfilling the primordial mandate.

In the New Beginning

Noah's story begins with creation having gone woefully awry. God's cosmic experiment has failed: the boundary between the divine and earthly realms is breached (Gen. 6:1-4), and violence pervades all creation (6:11). Whereas God planned that creation be filled with sustainable life, creation is now on the brink of self-destruction. Having hoped to see something of God's own self in human beings, cast in the divine "image," God now sees only evil inclinations (6:5). For whatever reason, creation has become hopelessly unsustainable. The state of the world, along with the state of the human heart, is in such bad shape that God regrets ever having created in the first place (6:6). God decides to finish (off) the world not out of anger but out of grief, for the world itself is bent on ecocide.[1] Call it cosmic euthanasia.

Yet God is not entirely done with (nor undone over) this cosmos project: God resolves to start over, to return to creation's formless beginning in order to create the world anew from its watery origins, cleansing it of its cancerous violence. But not completely: there is amid this cosmic experiment gone awry one sliver of success, one individual (and family) worth saving. He is the son of Lamech, whose birth name holds out hope for "relief" from the hard toil of working the cursed land (5:29). His name is Noah, the one who has "found favor in the LORD's sight" (6:8); righteous and blameless he is (6:9). As a man "out of the ground" (5:28; cf. 2:7),

---

1. The Hebrew word for "corrupt" in Gen. 6:11 comes from the same word as "destroy" in 6:13.

Noah is deemed the new Adam, for he holds the promise of creation's restoration, of creation's continuity between the old and the new.

Accompanying God's resolve to "destroy *all* flesh," flesh that has determined to destroy itself, is God's decision to save Noah and his family to preserve flesh in *all* its variety. Enter the ark, designed to preserve the land's biodiversity in the face of rising waters engulfing a world already engulfed by violence. The flood marks creation's reversion to its original state as the boundary separating the waters above from the waters below collapses (cf. 7:11 and 1:2, 6-8). Amid the surge of watery chaos, Noah, his family, and the animals ride out the storm to preserve the link between the old and the new. For all its chaos and catastrophe (see the movie), this scene can be viewed from another, more maternal perspective: the flooding of the earth marks creation's reentry into the womb; the waters that bear aloft the ark are akin to amniotic fluid, while the ark itself holds the promise of life's reproduction. The storm scene is also a womb scene.[2] Noah and the animals are on a re-creation mission. Cleansing the earth leads to the earth's rebirth.

Of all the human figures featured in the book of Genesis, Noah fulfills most fully the divine command to wield dominion over creation, and he does so by implementing God's first endangered species act. Once the land dries out, God repeats the primordial command to "be fruitful and multiply, and fill the earth" to Noah and his family (9:1; 1:28). Through Noah and his ark, creation is both preserved and renewed.

The Cosmic Covenant

Unlike the first time, creation this time comes complete with legal documentation: a covenant is established, the first ever. Genesis 9:8-17 formalizes God's cosmic restoration. Preceding it is a change of heart, God's heart. On the occasion of Noah's burnt offerings, God makes a solemn promise:

> I shall never again curse the ground because of humankind, for the inclination of the human heart is evil from youth. Nor shall I ever again

---

2. My thanks to Ralph C. Griffin for suggesting this alternative view. The flood scene as a womb scene highlights all the more God's personal investment in creation's renewal, both by covenant and by birth. It also imbues the scene described in Gen. 1:2 — the dark, watery conditions of precreation — with a womblike character (see chapter 1).

destroy every living creature as I have done. As long as the earth endures, seedtime and harvest, cold and heat, summer and winter, day and night, will not cease. (8:21-22)

God resolves never to destroy creation again, *despite* the human heart remaining "evil." For all its totalizing scope in purging the world of violence, the flood has not changed this one intractable feature of the human condition. While the earth has been cleansed, not so the human heart. Human beings, God concludes, remain trapped in their proclivity toward evil. It is this realization that prompted God to flood the earth in the first place (6:5). It is also this realization that now occasions the cosmic covenant. Whereas the human heart has not changed, God's heart has! God's cosmic concession is rooted in a heart bent toward forbearance. The movement of the seasons, the alternation of day and night, of planting and harvest, cold and heat: these seasonal shifts give sustaining testimony to God's resolve to "never again" destroy life in order to (re-)create life.

God's promise sets the stage for the covenant that follows, which opens with God blessing Noah and his family to replenish the earth (9:1), recalling the blessing given in Genesis 1:28. But something new is introduced: whereas the world of Genesis 1 assumed a vegetarian diet (1:29-30), God now allows for the eating of meat (9:2-3), a divine concession to humankind's flawed nature and, more practically, to the scarcity of edible plants following the flood. Such allowance is not without restriction, however: meat must be eaten without its blood, for blood is the sign of life (9:4). And while animal killing is allowed, the shedding of human blood is expressly forbidden (9:6a), the reason being humanity's own genesis, created in God's image (9:6b; cf. 1:26-28). Evil heart and divine image: such are the polarities of the human condition.

Such restrictions established in this postdiluvian world, however, cannot compare to the greatest restriction ever told, God's *self*-restriction! In Genesis 9:8-17, God promises to "never again" destroy "all flesh," indeed the earth itself, by the flood. Far different from a contractual agreement, God's covenant with Noah and the world is an unconditional promise, a unilateral decree that limits God's options toward the world. Divine destruction is now ruled out. The flood is deemed an unrepeatable event. In other words, God's covenant with Noah amounts to a self-restraining order. This covenant of restraint, moreover, is not limited to Noah and his family but applies to all the occupants of the ark, "all flesh."

God's first covenant in the Bible is a cosmic covenant, and the guarantee of its enforcement is a cosmic sign: the rainbow, an arresting sign of God's disarmament for future generations. We see a rainbow and marvel over its multicolored beauty caused by light refracted and reflected through water droplets. It is truly a wonder to behold. In the eyes of the biblical author, however, such an optical wonder points to a startling theological wonder. The narrator sees not a rainbow but a bow, God's composite bow, a weapon of war, and God has hung it in the clouds for good. Whenever God sees the bow, God will "remember" the covenant made on that new primordial day (9:15). For God, remembrance is not a matter of recollection, as if God could forget or grow senile. The Hebrew word for "remember" comes close to meaning "enact" or "fulfill" something as promised. The sign of the bow is a testimony that God has forever set aside the option of destruction as a way of dealing with creation. It is a sign that God is formally committed to divine disarmament. By freely hanging up the bow, God becomes covenantally bound to creation's welfare.

And so are we, for God's covenant with creation does not mean that God will prevent *us* from destroying the world with *our* weapons of destruction, from nuclear to carbon. To gaze at the rainbow through ancient eyes is to stare in wonder at the disarming beauty of God's covenantal commitment and to look forward in hope that we too may embody such covenantal resolve in our life-sustaining dominion, for our sake and for the world's sake. God's covenantal wonder is both an unexpected concession and an unprecedented commitment, a wonder that we are called to practice every time the rainbow is beheld.

4. *Woeful Wonder*

EXODUS 19–20

The people stood at a distance,
while Moses approached the thick darkness where God was.

Exodus 20:21

Israel's encounter with God at Mount Sinai is utterly wondrous but far from friendly. Frightening is more like it. The riveting scene that unfolds in Exodus 19 is an aw(e)ful display of divine power: God descends upon the mountain in a "dense cloud," with "thunder and lightning," "smoke," and "fire" accompanied by the piercing blasts of the *shofar* or ram's horn. Creation itself convulses in response to God's formal appearance, a theophany of terror. The people can only "tremble" in response. So should the reader, whom the text grabs and throws headlong into the fray of God's holy presence. Survival is not assured.

Neither is clarity: Exodus 19–20 is a woefully convoluted text. It's difficult, for example, to keep track of how many times Moses climbs up and down the mountain (e.g., 19:9, 14). When you think Moses has come down, he's back up again, and vice versa. Throughout the narrative Moses is an ever moving target, ascending and descending like the angels on Jacob's staircase (not a "ladder"; Gen. 28:12). And not just Moses: at one moment the people are barred from touching the mountain, and in the next they are allowed to "go up on the mountain" (Exod. 19:12-13). Despite its convoluted nature, however, the text of Exodus 19–20 does share a consistency of theme: holy fear and fascination. Unlike in the garden of Eden (Gen.

47

3:8), there is nothing casual about Israel's encounter on the mountain. The account is filled with images of terror and transcendence. And so God's appearance on the mountain requires stringent preparations on the part of the people: boundaries are set and the people are consecrated. God's holy presence tolerates no illicit contact. Both the mountain and the women are deemed untouchable (19:12-13, 15). On the third day, cloud and smoke envelop the mountain. Deuteronomy recalls the mountain as "ablaze with fire up to the heart of the heavens, shrouded in darkness, cloud, and gloom" (Deut. 4:11). Only Moses and later Aaron are allowed to ascend to the top where God has descended "in fire" (Exod. 19:18-20).

The Visible Voice

On the mountain, God's appearance is a feast to both eyes and ears, but in the end it is the visual that serves the verbal. The pyrotechnical display sets the stage for God's public address to all Israel, the Decalogue (Exod. 20:1-17; Deut. 4:13), the sound of which establishes its own commanding presence. According to Deuteronomy, in fact, only the voice of God is perceived, albeit a voice "out of the fire" (Deut. 4:12, 15), a voice that the gathered people can withstand only so long. According to one ancient testimony in Exodus, not only did the Israelites hear the thunderous voice of God, they *saw* it. An ancient Greek version of Exodus 20:18a literally reads, "And all the people saw the voice," which in the Hebrew text as we have it is cast in the plural, usually taken to mean lightning bolts.[1] But in the Greek version, God's voice takes on color; it is a visible voice. One can only imagine what God's voice may have sounded like, let alone what it may have *looked* like! One stream of Jewish thought imagined God's voice as flames of fire striking the tablets.[2]

For all the visual effects of God's presence on the mountaintop, it is the voice that carries the day, the voice that thunders out the Decalogue. It is the voice that the people "see" (20:18-19). But regardless of its visual form, God's voice proves to be too much; the people confess to not be-

1. The Septuagint or Old Greek version likely preserves the older reading. See Azzan Yadin, "*Qôl* as Hypostasis in the Hebrew Bible," *Journal of Biblical Literature* 122 (2003): 601-26 at 617-23.

2. Attributed to Rabbi Akiba in *Mekhilta de-Rabbi Ishmael*, ed. Jacob Z. Lauterbach (Philadelphia: Jewish Publication Society, 2004), 2.338. The midrash goes on to imagine the Israelites able to immediately interpret the visible words ushering from God's mouth.

ing able to endure, verbally and visually, the voice behind the Decalogue. Hence, the people elect Moses to mediate the remainder of God's words after the Decalogue's public pronouncement. On the mountain, the divine voice points to divine presence seamlessly conceived as terrifyingly transcendent, requiring the people to stand at a distance and be consecrated.

Virulent Holiness

Holiness takes a front seat at Sinai. The theophany at Sinai vividly illustrates Rudolf Otto's famous notion of the holy as *mysterium tremendum et fascinans,* as fearful and fascinating mystery.[3] The narrative exemplifies this in the way both Moses and the people respond to God's presence on the mountain. The people are warned not "to go up the mountain or to touch the edge of it"; otherwise, they will "be put to death" (19:12). God later tells Moses to warn the "people not to break through to the LORD to look; otherwise many of them will perish" (19:21). The verb "break through" *(hsr)* suggests a violent act. Elsewhere, it refers to the "breaking down" or "tearing down" of walls, altars, and cities (Judg. 6:25; 1 Kings 18:30; Ezek. 13:14; 26:12; Prov. 14:1). Such violence will be met by force, God warns: God will "break out" or burst forth *(prts)* against the people in response (Exod. 19:21, 24), perhaps like a plague (Ps. 106:29). Holiness, in other words, threatens to unleash a divine virulence if boundaries are breached through careless action. Due to God's descent, the mountain has become something like a hot zone of contagion or, to use another analogy, aglow with radioactive intensity. Anyone who gets contaminated dies. The sound of the *shofar,* then, is akin to the piercing blasts of a siren warning of deadly threat.

Such stringent orders not only point to God's desire to remain set apart from the people; they also acknowledge the people's illicit desire to "go up" and approach God — or, better, rush God — eager to get a piece of the deity. The narrative implicates the people's desire to draw near (Exod. 19:21) as reckless, as a rapacious desire to know God, not unlike the "men of Sodom" who wanted to "know" the angelic visitors (Gen. 19:4-5). Access denied.

---

3. Rudolf Otto, *The Idea of the Holy: An Inquiry into the Non-rational Factor in the Idea of the Divine and Its Relation to the Rational* (New York: Oxford University Press, 1958), esp. 12-40.

Nevertheless, this event of *tremendum,* with all its precautions, dire warnings, and pyrotechnic terror, is meant to facilitate a way for the people "to meet God" safely (Exod. 19:17). They are permitted to "go up on the mountain" at the sound of the *shofar* (19:13), to approach God on cue not just with fear and trembling but also, one might say, decently and in order. The priests are allowed to approach God if and only if they "consecrate themselves," that is, make themselves holy (19:22). Indeed, consecration is mandatory. Through it, the people, particularly the priests, come to share in some attenuated way an aspect of the divine and are thereby protected from the full brunt of God's holiness. Consecration is akin to vaccination: diluted or benign holiness is administered to build up protection against the ultimate source of holiness, God. But it only works so far. The movements of the priests remain limited before God (19:24). No one has unfettered access to God except Moses. He is up on top of the mountain while the people are gathered far down below. Moses ascends to God and remains with God, having accessed the seemingly inaccessible. How so? Is it because Moses has built up a natural resistance to holiness? Has he been doubly vaccinated/consecrated? The text does not suggest this; it simply indicates that he has been chosen. Drawn fearfully to the burning bush sixteen chapters earlier (see below), on the same mountain no less (3:1, 12), Moses is now appointed as God's spokesperson and the people's mediator (20:19, 22). From burning bush to burning mountain, God's *mysterium tremendum* moves from private to public, and so also Moses' affiliation with God, now in full display.

Facilitating Fear and Affiliation

The narrative walks a fine, if zigzaggy, line between keeping distance from and approaching near to God, between fear and fascination regarding God's presence. On the one hand, the people "tremble" at a distance before God's magisterial presence. On the other hand, they are restive, moved by transgressive desire. In its own dramatic way, the narrative captures something of the inner tension of holy presence. Holiness both repels and attracts; it threatens and arouses, this woeful wonder. The dialectic of distance and approach, of fear and fascination, setting apart and setting in relationship, permission and restraint, dread and desire are all woven into this complex narrative driven by the paradox of holiness.

In the end, however, holiness presents a way forward: it facilitates a way for a people to be claimed by God as a "priestly kingdom and a holy nation," categorically distinct from the other nations (19:6). Distinction-making is based on relationship building, and it is difficult and dangerous work, the narrative claims. For all the sound and fury on the mountain, it is God's aim to make Israel "my treasured possession out of all the peoples" (19:5). It is God's desire to establish a covenantal bond with a band of former slaves, and God does so with a volcanic explosion of holiness that radiates a mountain and infects a people while also ensuring their survival from a distance.

God's public appearance is, moreover, meant to sear permanently into a people's collective memory God's power to initiate a relationship and motivate obedience, to "instill the fear of [God] so that you do not sin" (20:20). As Deuteronomy puts it, such an experience constitutes a teachable moment: "So that they may learn to fear me as long as they live on earth, and may teach their children so" (4:10). According to Rudolf Otto, an awareness of the numinous "cannot, strictly speaking, be taught; it can only be evoked, awakened in the mind."[4] Not so according to Deuteronomy: the "fear of the LORD" is a *learned* fear, a fear that is teachable from generation to generation in the retelling of the mountain experience and in the reciting of the law, both held inseparably together at Sinai (or Horeb — the name of the mountain according to Deuteronomy). Such "fear," the "fear of the LORD," is the beginning of obedience, and obedience, in turn, is a matter of practicing wonder.

Terrible Wonder

The story of God's descent upon the mountain and before a people illustrates well the fine line between terror and wonder. In this account, both share a common starting point. Which one wins is ultimately decided by the story's outcome. If the people are destroyed in this encounter, then it is all for naught: terror wins. But they survive. Like the burning bush the people remain unconsumed by God's fiery presence on the mountain. Although survival in the face of grave threat is essential, it is not sufficient. The people are not paralyzed but reconstituted, transformed. And that's what makes this account a text of wonder. All this woeful wonder is about forming a community, specifically a community whose constitution is

---

4. Otto, *The Idea of the Holy*, 7.

firmly established in the fire and the law, in the terror and the *torah*. What is determinative of wonder, as opposed to outright terror, is not just the survival of a people but the formation of community.

It has been said that it took the ten plagues to get Israel out of Egypt; now it takes the Ten Commandments to keep Egypt out of Israel, to turn a band of erstwhile slaves, ever longing for the "fleshpots" of Egypt, into a fully constituted community ready to move forward with God. In other words, only in God's delivery of the *torah* is full deliverance of a people attained. Beginning with the Decalogue, the law plays an indispensable role in a people's transformation, from slavery to freedom to community. The voice says it all from the outset: "I am the LORD your God, who brought you out of the land of Egypt, out of the house of slavery; you shall have no other gods before me" (Exod. 20:2-3). God's fearsome, saving presence points to God's commanding, guiding word. Through their fearful encounter with God's presence and through their willing reception of God's word, the people are born again, transformed into a community of obedience. Wonder is the midwife.

Theophanies in Miniature

The Sinai encounter with the divine is framed by two other, more intimate encounters: the burning bush scene sixteen chapters earlier and the "glory" episode fourteen chapters later. Both involve Moses one-on-one with God.

The Burning Bush

The burning bush begins the episode of Moses' mission, and it opens with a distraction that causes Moses to "turn aside" (Exod. 3:3-4): an unburned flaming bush, a sight caught in a shepherd's peripheral vision. But in the larger framework of the Moses story, stretching back to the beginning of Exodus, the burning bush is a distraction within a much larger distraction.[5] Far way in the land of Midian, Moses has turned aside from his own people, who remain enslaved in Egypt. This distraction on the mountain, it turns out, will take him back to where he began and where he should be. As

---

5. Well noted by Ralph C. Griffin.

Moses the shepherd turns aside to get a closer look, simple curiosity turns to fearful awe when a voice out of the fire calls his name, stopping him in his tracks. He is on "holy ground" and thus must remove his sandals. A shepherd's sandals carry dirt, including sheep dung, evidently not allowed on sacred soil. But by taking off his sandals, Moses becomes intimately in touch with the divine and, consequently, grounded in a new calling. What is it like to touch holiness between one's toes, to feel the sacred soil beneath one's bare feet? Tingly, electrifying, soothing? However it must have felt, Moses stands exposed before God, in touch with God, and becomes contaminated with holiness. He is about to be consumed with God's passion for a people, his people. This turning aside, it turns out, marks Moses' return to his people and eventually his return back to the mountain of the burning bush, Sinai. By then Moses will be bringing his people instead of his sheep. By then an entire mountain will be ablaze with God's presence.

The voice identifies the speaker as the God of the ancestral past now roused by the cries of the oppressed. This holy God is moved by the pain of "my people" (3:7). God is inflamed with the passion to deliver a people from bondage, a divine passion that eventually kindles the heart of a reluctant refugee. What about the burning bush itself? More than a bright ornament designed to catch Moses' attention, this extraordinary image is fraught with symbolic import. The bush itself is much more than an object of curiosity. In it one sees the flaming heart of God conjoined to the suffering state of God's people, enslaved but not consumed. Israel enslaved, Israel invaded, Israel in exile, Israel occupied. Why is the bush not "burned up"? Moses asks. A corollary question is, "Why are God's people not extinguished?" A cause for wonderment.

The Backside of Glory

On the other side of Sinai is another encounter with the divine, this time involving God's exposure to Moses, a sort of reversal of the burning bush episode. At the renewal of the covenant following the golden calf debacle is the intimate narrative concerning God's glory revealed to Moses. A private conversation unfolds between God and Moses. In the "tent of meeting," Moses and God have been speaking "face to face" as friends typically do (33:11). But now Moses has a request. Relying on God's favor, Moses demands to see God's "glory" (33:18). "Glory" in Hebrew *(kabod)* literally means weight, and so divine glory is something that no one can bear. So

God can agree to Moses' demand only partially. In God's "face," the fullness of divine glory shines, but in God's passing backside, Moses can catch at least a glimpse, pushing the limits of what he can endure.

After Moses has cut two new tablets and heads up the mountain (again!), God descends "in the cloud" and passes before Moses pronouncing the sacred name, YHWH ("LORD"; 34:5; cf. 3:13-16). But what is most revealing is not what is seen but what is said. As in Exodus 19–20, the voice takes precedence over the visual. Amid God's passing and partial glory, Moses receives a full revelation of God's character: merciful and gracious, abounding in faithful love *(chesed),* slow to anger, forgiving sin to the "thousandth generation" yet holding the guilty accountable to the "third and the fourth generation" (34:6-7). God has exposed far more than a backside. God's very heart is laid bare in word. It is God's self-confession.

God's exposure to Moses marks the high point, the revelatory pinnacle, of God's presence in the Pentateuch, if not the entire Hebrew Bible. It is no coincidence that this divine confession is dispersed throughout the Bible, from the Prophets to the Writings.[6] On the mountain, the veil is lifted to reveal God's grace and mercy, love and faithfulness, forgiveness and justice. Curiously, however, such revelation makes no mention of holiness. "Glory," instead, commands the attention, and in glory God's compassionate character is unveiled, a compassion exercised in protecting Moses and in accompanying a "stiff-necked" people (34:8). Therein lies a mystery as wondrous as a burning bush.

Elusive Presence, Explosive Passion

In Exodus, and throughout the Bible, God becomes increasingly complex in character: hidden and revealed, concealed and exposed, hence the opposing images of light and darkness that enshrine the deity, from dark clouds to blazing light (e.g., Deut. 4:10-11). God is "enwrapped with light as with a garment" (Ps. 104:2) yet resides in "thick darkness" in the temple's inner sanctum (1 Kings 8:12) and on the top of a mountain (Exod. 20:21). Such contrasting shades mark, indeed ensure, God's "elusive presence."[7]

---

6. But also repeatedly throughout the Hebrew Scriptures with slight variation: see Num. 14:18; Neh. 9:17, 31; Ps. 86:15; 103:8; 145:8; Joel 2:13; Nah. 1:3; Jonah 4:2.

7. As Samuel Terrien aptly coins in *The Elusive Presence: Toward a New Biblical Theology,* Religious Perspectives 26 (San Francisco: Harper & Row, 1978).

In theophany accounts beyond Sinai, most of them cast poetically, the comingling of light and darkness persists: God's nostrils breathe out smoke, and fire issues forth from God's mouth, for example, in Psalm 18:8. Fire and heavy clouds, lighting and thunder, hail and coals: all are marks of a God-awful storm. Two verses are particularly vivid:

> He made darkness his covering all around him;
>   his canopy was dark waters and dense clouds.
> From the brightness before him his clouds broke out,
>   with hail and coals of fire. (Ps. 18:11-12)

In Psalm 97, "clouds and thick darkness" surround God as "fire goes before him" with the people beholding "his glory" (97:6). Habakkuk exults in God's "glory," evident in shafts of light and in "brightness like the sun" (3:4). Such searing images of divine power are unleashed once a cry is heard by God. The terrifying theophany depicted in Psalm 18 erupts when the speaker calls "upon the LORD for help" (18:6). In Exodus, a bush burns because God has "heard their cry" (3:7). God has caught wind of their "groanings" (2:23-24), and the flames are fanned. The prophet Habakkuk declares that God's harnessed fury was for saving a people in the exodus (Hab. 3:13) and counts it as a precedent for what God can do now on behalf of his people: "In our time revive it," the prophet cries to God (3:2). The cry for deliverance kindles God's holy heart, and the world is set aflame. "Holy, holy, holy is the LORD of hosts; the whole earth is full of God's glory!" (Isa. 6:3). God's perfect storm reflects a sublime passion for those in dire straits, for it is in response to great need that God's glory, God's power and might, God's inflamed presence, becomes most fully manifest. God's saving glory is set in reply to the human cry of woe: such is God's "woeful" wonder.

5. *Playful Wonder*

PROVERBS 8:22-31

I was daily his delight, playing before him every moment.

Proverbs 8:30b

One of the most exquisitely crafted poems in all of Scripture is found in Proverbs 8:22-31, a singularly evocative passage that has captivated readers for centuries, from ancient sages to contemporary feminists and even ecologists. The poem has also been fought over in the christological disputes of the early church and the theological controversies of the present. Through no fault of its own, the text bears a rather bruised legacy. Poetry is not well suited for settling heated theological debates. The challenge is to look beyond the poem's battle scars and welcome its wonder with eyes wide open, delighting in its richness, come what may.

> The LORD created me as the beginning of his work,
>> the first of his primordial acts.
> Of old I was woven, from the very beginning,
>> even before the earth itself.
> When the deeps were not existent, I was given birth.
>> When the wellsprings were not yet laden with water,
>>> when the mountains were not yet anchored,
>>>> before the hills themselves, I was brought forth.
> Before the LORD made the earth abroad, and the first bits of soil,
>> when the LORD established the heavens, I was there.

When the LORD circumscribed the surface of the deep,
   when the LORD secured the skies,
   and stabilized the springs of the deep,
   when the LORD assigned the sea its limit
     (lest the waters transgress God's decree),
   when the LORD inscribed the foundations of the earth,
   I was beside him growing up.
I was daily his delight, playing before him every moment.
   playing with his inhabited world,
     delighting in the offspring of *adam.*

Proverbs 8:22-31 is a creation account unlike any other. The poem lingers over God at work in the methodical construction of the cosmos, step by step, "when" by "when." But this account is punctuated repeatedly by an "I," an eyewitness who turns this cosmic litany into a personal testimony. This cosmic poem, it turns out, is a soliloquy of self-praise designed to woo the reader with Wisdom's wonder.

Woman Wisdom

Who is this self-appointed speaker, making such bold claims about herself? She is Wisdom with a capital W, the archetypal personification of God's wisdom: feminine, cosmic, prophetic, maternal, and, as we shall see, childlike. She addresses her audience both as her lovers and as her children. Wisdom condemns as easily as she commends (Prov. 1:20-33). She can be fearsome and demanding, as well as gentle and comforting. In 8:22-31, at the pinnacle of her discourse, Wisdom proves to be disarmingly delightful and formidably persuasive. Here she lifts her voice above the fray of conflicting voices featured throughout the first nine chapters of the book, all of them vying for attention (e.g., Prov. 1:11-14; 7:14-20; 9:13-18), to convince her audience of her worthiness in the world, and she does so by infectiously sharing the joy of her preeminent position in relation to God and the world. By claiming an intimate, playful association with both creation and creator, Wisdom hopes to capture our allegiance by captivating our imagination.

    Modesty does not become Wisdom. Her discourse is replete with self-assertion. "The LORD created *me*" (8:22); "*I* was woven at the very beginning" (8:23); "*I* was given birth" (8:24, 25); "*I* was beside him" (8:30);

"*I* was God's delight" (8:30). Although her speech focuses resolutely on God's work in creation, repeated references to herself nearly match her references to the creator. When it comes to God and creation, Wisdom essentially says, "Hello! It's all about *me!*" In self-praise, Wisdom sets herself over all her competitors.[1] Imagine Wisdom in a beauty pageant. Her worth? Beyond compare (8:10-11). Her vocation? Teaching (a most noble profession; 8:15-16; 9:1-6). "The way of righteousness" and "justice" is her runway (8:20). Her pedigree? She is God's only begotten daughter (8:23-25, 30-31). Wisdom wins! Her rivals never had a chance.

The poem of Proverbs 8:22-31 is all about establishing Wisdom's preeminence, cosmically and personally. According to her testimony, Wisdom was birthed prior to the rest of creation. Her speech charts her own development and growth: she was conceived (8:22), gestated (8:23), birthed (8:24-25), present before creation (8:27), and growing up and playing (8:30-31). In Proverbs 8, the world's creation is told strictly from the standpoint of Wisdom's "genetic" primacy. Whereas her origin is sharply distinguished from the origins of the cosmos, Wisdom shares an intimate bond with the "inhabited world" (8:31). Indeed, Wisdom requires a world in order to be wise.

World-Play

What kind of world does Wisdom require? It is a world that *everyone* requires in order to flourish, a world that is stable and secure, as well as engaging and enthralling. Wisdom recounts God at work in carving, anchoring, stabilizing, establishing, circumscribing, and securing creation. The mountains serve as weight-bearing pillars holding up the heavens to prevent cosmic collapse. Boundaries are set to limit the sea from overwhelming the land. A "circle" is drawn upon "the face of the deep," and the "foundations of the earth" are laid with exacting measurements. God the architect constructs a universe that is safe and secure. God sets the cosmic infrastructures and boundaries firmly in place, all to maintain the world's stability. It is a world carefully designed for someone. But for whom?

---

1. Her main competitor in Proverbs is the so-called strange woman, featured particularly in Prov. 7:6-27. For more discussion about Wisdom's voice among the other voices of Proverbs, see William P. Brown, *Wisdom's Wonder: Character, Creation, and Crisis in the Bible's Wisdom Literature* (Grand Rapids: Eerdmans, 2014), 41-49.

Except for the glancing reference in the final verse, absent is any specific reference to the creation of life, human or otherwise, in Wisdom's grand soliloquy. The cosmos is mostly bricks and mortar, with life only a lingering by-product. But not quite. The poem acknowledges something vibrantly alive in and beyond the world: Wisdom. In relation to her, God is not just the creator of the cosmos. The deity of design is also a doting, playful (not to mention single) parent! Wisdom is God's very daughter, no less, and the entire world is her playhouse. For God so loved Wisdom that he gave the world to his only begotten daughter, so that she would become wise. Thus the wondrous paradox of Wisdom as child in this poem: Wisdom grows in wisdom.

Even as a child, Wisdom is no passive observer. Although the poem nowhere suggests that Wisdom collaborates with God in the work of cosmic construction, she is no mere spectator. Wisdom makes her own contribution to the cosmos, but it has nothing to do with infrastructure or design. She provides play.

> When the LORD inscribed the foundations of the earth,
>   I was beside him growing up.[2]
> I have been daily his delight,
>   playing before him every moment,
> playing with his inhabited world,
>   delighting in the offspring of *adam*. (8:29b-31)

In her relationship to the world, Wisdom is a child, watching, playing, and delighting. Her play, in fact, serves double duty. Wisdom engages both God and the world in mutual play, holding creator and creation together through the common bond of joy. As the subject of God's delight, Wisdom is "de-light of the world" that enlightens the world. Here, Wisdom's legacy is levity.

In this poem, Wisdom is created in the image of the playing child

---

2. This is a much disputed line that hangs on the meaning of one puzzling word in Hebrew *(amon)*. Contrary to most Bible translations, the grammatical form of the word appears to be verbal, specifically an infinitive absolute of *'mn*, "to support" or "nourish" (see the same verb in Esth. 2:20b). The larger context, moreover, tips the scale. Given the absence of any hint of creative activity on Wisdom's part in the poem, contra the New Revised Standard Version's "master worker," coupled with the theme of play immediately following, the image of Wisdom as a child fits the immediate context best. For detailed argumentation, see Michael V. Fox, "'*Āmôn* Again," *Journal of Biblical Literature* 115 (1996): 699-702.

(imago nati), an image underappreciated by many interpreters, such as the notable wisdom scholar R. B. Y. Scott, who felt that "the imagery of a gay, thoughtless childhood is inappropriate" in light of Wisdom's "primacy in creation" and her "high claim to grave authority" in the poem.[3] But are cosmological "primacy" and exuberant play mutually exclusive? Scott does not appreciate that Wisdom's discourse is pure poetry and that poetry can hold together what logic tries to pull apart. Moreover, the poetic convergence of primacy and play is rhetorically significant: it is precisely as a child that Wisdom forges a uniquely intimate bond with God, with creation, and with the reader. As every reader was once a child, so also Wisdom, God's child.[4] Wisdom recounts her childhood with God and the world, and in so doing celebrates her primacy in God and over the world. The authority that Wisdom embodies is not so much "grave" as it is creative, playfully creative, an authority grounded in cosmic intimacy, an authority that is more generative than restrictive, more relational than referential. The image of playful, childlike Wisdom is no superficial metaphor. Indeed, Wisdom's very words, beginning in 8:22, can be read as the words of a child asserting her unique, rightful relationship with God as firstborn, indeed the firstborn of all creation, with all creation made for her play. The cosmos is, as it were, "childproofed" by God, or better, made child friendly, fully conducive for her growth and enjoyment. Wisdom is God's cosmic child encountering the world in gleeful delight. She is the world's first explorer, Wisdom the wonderer.

Wisdom's testimony is all about her joy to the world and to God. God has given her birth and nurtured her growth to take delight in her cosmic home. Playful Wisdom, thus, is no mere instrument or attribute of God's creative abilities (cf. 3:19). According to the sages, Wisdom is God's full partner in play, and all creation is hers to enjoy. The world was made for Wisdom, for her flourishing and delight, and it is in utter delight that she embraces the world. As a child grows in wisdom by playfully exploring her environment, so Wisdom delightfully engages creation. It is fun to imagine what could prompt Wisdom's exuberant delight in the world, what might pique her curiosity about the world. Does her joy stem from discovering the world's wondrous complexities, from quarks to quasars? Does she

---

3. R. B. Y. Scott, "Wisdom in Creation: The *'Āmôn* of Proverbs viii 30," *Vetus Testamentum* 10 (1960): 213-23 at 218-19.

4. Indeed, Prov. 1–9 rhetorically casts the reader as a child, literally a "son" (e.g., 1:8, 10, 15; 2:1; 3:1, 11; 4:1, 10, 20; 7:1).

have a special fondness for its marvelous, most complex inhabitants? Who else, in addition to the "offspring of *adam,*" occupies creation for the sake of Wisdom's delight? Perhaps frolicking coneys, roaring lions, breaching whales, and flapping ostriches (see chapters 6–7)? They, too, inhabit creation, and thus have a right to play with Wisdom. And then there is God, with whom Wisdom shares a special relationship. As God's partner in play, she is "beside" the creator of all as much as she is beside herself in joy. The pleasure of play, an inherently shared enterprise, suffuses Wisdom's growth "at every moment."

To revel in Wisdom's world is to experience the joy of discovery, the delight of discernment, and the thrill of edifying play. To live in Wisdom's world, the sages say elsewhere, is to walk the path she forges, the path of "righteousness, justice, and equity" (Prov. 1:3), a path that "is like the light of dawn, shining brighter and brighter until full day" (4:18). Wisdom's path is the journey of discernment in which what is discovered and what is revealed are one and the same. But the "full day" that ushers in all knowledge and insight, the sages acknowledge, never truly arrives. The aged always have more to learn (1:5). As Wisdom's growth begins and continues in joy, may the wide-eyed wonder of children never be lost on the wise. In Wisdom's eyes, there are no grownups, at least "grownups" who have learned it all. The quest for wisdom is ever ongoing, and progress on the path will always be marked with baby steps. In Wisdom, we are all beginners and will remain ever so.

Childlike Wisdom

To conclude, I turn to the text in another way. To engage children with the Bible, it is easy to have them repeat paraphrases and variations of the text said out loud, a sort of "Simon says" with Scripture but without the "gotcha" part.[5] No knowledge of reading is required, for anyone can repeat and recite. Reciting, in fact, was the standard practice of reading Scripture in antiquity. In ancient times, reading was always performative, never silent or passive. Below is an example of "reading" Proverbs 8:22-31 whereby each line is read by the leader and then repeated by children.

---

5. I am indebted to Christian educator Paul Osborne for demonstrating this in worship with another text.

In the beginning God created me.
God created me.
Me!
ME!

I was woven from the very beginning,
woven,
woven in the womb.

Before the Big Bang, I was birthed.
Before earth and all stars,
before the hills were set in place,
I was born.

Before the moon kindled the darkness,
before the wind kindled the fire,
before the rain filled every ocean,

I was there.
There I was!
And there, and there, and there!

I was beside God growing up,
growing and developing,
nurtured and loved,
growing in God's ways.

I was God's delight day by day,
day by day,
day by day (sung).

I was the de-light of the world,
playing and dancing,
dancing and delighting,

Playing in God's wondrous world,
in God's world of wonders!

Playing with the children of Adam and Eve,
with lions and tigers and bears.

Oh my!
   Amen!
Let's play!

Actually, it works just as well with adults.

6. Manifold Wonder

PSALM 104

How many are your works, O LORD! You have made them all
  in wisdom.
The earth is stock full of your creatures!

Psalm 104:24

John Calvin (1509-64), that austere and resolute founder of the Reformed tradition, had a favorite verse in Psalm 104. But it wasn't the verse you might expect. It's not the one that refers to God resplendently wrapped in light (104:2). Neither is it the one describing God's thunderous rebuke against the waters (104:7), nor is it the psalmist's call to destroy the wicked (104:35a). No, Calvin's favorite verse was the one that begins: "Wine to gladden the human heart" (104:15).[1] Calvin found a kindred spirit in the ancient psalmist. Both the reformer and the sage were intoxicated with creation's wonder.

The Wonderful

The psalmist praises God for the grape, the olive, and the grain, the prime agricultural products of the Fertile Crescent of his day. Wine, oil, and

---

1. It is the one verse he wrote the most about in the psalm; see John Calvin, *Commentary on the Book of Psalms,* trans. James Anderson (Grand Rapids: Baker, 1979), 6.155-58.

bread are, as Calvin put it, signs of God's "superabundant liberality,"[2] signs of God's joyful generosity in creation. Such joy undergirds this poetic celebration of creation, from beginning to the end, with one exception (see below). The psalm not only describes joy, it prescribes joy, for us and for God.

Psalm 104 begins with riveting imagery of God enwrapped with light vigorously unfurling the cosmos like fabric, complete with gravitational waves.[3] The psalm concludes, nearly so, with the speaker exhorting God to celebrate creation: "May the LORD rejoice in his works" (104:31b). This is a rather surprising turn: the psalmist is bold enough to exhort *God* to rejoice, not just God's creatures. The language of unabashed joy is rarely attributed to God in the Bible. Psalm 104 is an unqualified exception.

The poetry of the psalm is crafted with a purpose, specifically to provide warrant for God's enjoyment of creation, as if God needed reason to do so. But such is the poetry's aim. This psalm offers specific reasons why God should enjoy creation, and the main one is creation's diversity. "How many are your works, O LORD! You have made them all in wisdom. The earth is stock full of your creatures!" (104:24). The psalmist is "seized with astonishment," to borrow from Calvin,[4] or gripped with wonder by the sheer variety of life on earth. The result is a poetic revelry in creation's diversity. The psalm lovingly details an array of animals and their habitats; each is quite different, yet each is part of an interconnected, flourishing whole. The psalm offers an infectiously joyous portrayal of the natural world with a special focus on the wilderness, traditionally considered a place of chaos. Instead of "lions and tigers and bears, O my!" the psalm proclaims, "Lions and tigers and bears, amen!" The psalmist rejoices in the richly diverse animal planet and in the God who sustains it all in joy.[5]

In its grand panoramic sweep, the psalm deftly covers everything from the theological and the cosmological to the ecological and the biological, all bracketed by the doxological. But in its coverage of creation, the psalm sets its sights primarily on the botanical and the zoological: cedars, fir trees, mountain goats, storks, coneys (or hyraxes), lions, and Leviathan

---

2. Calvin, *Commentary on the Book of Psalms,* 6.155.

3. This is one way of imagining gravitational waves caused by the Big Bang, recently observed by astrophysicists!

4. Calvin, *Psalms,* 6.164.

5. For a detailed discussion of Ps. 104 in relation to biology and ecology, see William P. Brown, *The Seven Pillars of Creation: The Bible, Science, and the Ecology of Wonder* (New York: Oxford University Press, 2010), 141-59.

all populate the world of the psalm, and all are lovingly detailed in a tone of rapturous praise to the creator. Even the trees have standing in Psalm 104:

> The trees of the LORD are well watered;
>   the cedars of Lebanon that the LORD planted.
> There the birds build their nests;
>   the stork has its home in the fir trees. (104:16-17; cf. 104:12)

The psalmist lingers admiringly over the mighty cedars of Lebanon, whose timber was a highly prized commodity among the mighty empires of ancient times. Armies from Mesopotamia would march westward, conquering cities and territories in their path, to get to the cedar forests near the Mediterranean seaboard, cut them down, and use the lumber for constructing their monumental palaces and temples. These trees once grew in dense forests on the slopes of Lebanon's mountains. Few remain today.

The psalmist, however, cherishes these trees not for their lumber but for their majesty and their accommodating capacity. The towering cedars are for the birds! This seemingly minor reference is actually crucial to appreciating the psalmist's view of creation as a whole. Most commentators identify the central theme of provision in the psalm, and appropriately so. God provides drink to the wild animals (104:11), "waters the mountains" and "the trees" (104:13, 16), causes "grass to grow for the cattle" (104:14), provides bread, wine, and oil for human beings (104:15), and supplies "prey" for the lions (104:21) as well as food for all creatures "in due season" (104:27). Providing for life is part of God's ongoing work of creation. Such is the creator's passion.

But in addition to provision, there is another crucial feature in the psalm, for which the majestic cedars offer but one example. The clue lies in God's first act of creation. In the beginning God created a heavenly home, a habitat for divinity, and in turn established domiciles for every living creature: streams and trees for the birds (104:12, 17), mountains for the wild goats (104:18a), and rocks for the coneys (104:18b). Even the waters have their "appointed" place (104:8-9). The lions have their dens, just as humans have their homes (104:26). The earth is not just a habitat for humanity but a habitat for all living kind, a habitat for diversity: "The earth is stock full of your creatures!" (104:24).

Indeed, human beings are scarcely mentioned at all until 104:23 (cf. 104:14-15), and only then along with the lions. The only difference between humans and lions within the created order, according to 104:20-23, is that the lions take the night shift to pursue their living, whereas humans go forth during the day to their labors. Day and night, the diurnal and the nocturnal, are part of creation's natural rhythm, a rhythm in which each species has its time as much as each has its place. The earth was created specifically to accommodate life in all its sheer variety.

But of all the creatures admired in the psalm, there is one that seems to inspire God's joy the most, a creature that elicits a special divine fondness. And like Calvin's favorite verse, this divinely favored creature is not one you might expect:

> There is the sea,
>> both vast and wide . . .
> There go the ships,
>> and, *voila,* there's Leviathan,
>> which you fashioned to play with![6] (104:25-26)

The vast sea accommodates a multitude of living beings, including the greatest of them all, Leviathan, the monster of the deep. Leviathan's reputation as a denizen of chaos precedes its appearance in Psalm 104. Elsewhere in biblical tradition, Leviathan is a multiheaded Hydra, God's mortal enemy destined for destruction (Ps. 74:12-14; Isa. 27:1). A terror-inspiring description of Leviathan can be found in Job 41. It is a creature clearly not for play but for combat, and its defeat is deemed an urgent necessity for creation's sake. But not in our psalm (nor in Job, as we shall see). No hint of horror is present in Psalm 104. God's alleged enemy turns out to be God's playmate. What the psalmist has done through the power of poetry is take a thing of abject terror and turn it into an object of playful wonder. In the poet's hands, Leviathan the monster of the deep becomes Leviathan God's partner in play! Just imagine God and Leviathan frolicking together in the ocean. Still, I for one would want to keep my distance.

As for humankind in this psalm, we are simply one species among many, and that too is a wonder. Creation is a shared habitation, and if there is a perfection or ideal presumed in the psalmist's world, it is the perfection of biodiversity, the wild and wondrous diversity of life and habitat. By

---

6. The syntax is ambiguous, given the possible antecedents for the suffixed preposition *bô*. Thus, the text could be translated: "Leviathan, which you fashioned to play in it [the sea]" (so New Revised Standard Version). But this possibility is less likely in view of the syntactical proximity of "Leviathan" in the verse.

listing various animal species, the psalmist offers a selective sample of the vast Encyclopedia of Life, which continues to be catalogued day by day (www.eol.org). As the species of life are varied and numerous, so also are their niches, from towering trees and flowing wadis to mountainous crags and the deep dark sea. In God's cosmic mansion there are many dwelling places, each fit for each species. Humanity's place in the varied order of creation is as legitimate as that of any other species, along with the coney and the onager ("wild ass"). There is living room for all.

The great evolutionary biologist J. B. S. Haldane (1892-1964) was asked by a cleric what biology could say about God. He allegedly replied, "I'm really not sure, except that the Creator, if he exists, must have an inordinate fondness of beetles."[7] Indeed, beetles, with their 400,000 species, make up close to 25 percent of all known animal species.[8] But whether beetles or Behemoths, God loves them all, God the biophile.

The Wicked

But for all of the psalm's celebration of nature's wondrous goodness, its beauty and bounty, the psalm ends on a resoundingly sour note. There is something wicked in the land of "lions and tigers and bears, amen!" In the last verse, the psalmist exhorts God to vanquish the wicked (104:35a). The psalm's cosmic scope, which includes even the monstrous Leviathan within the orbit of God's providential care, has no room for the wicked. For some readers, the call to destroy sinners in the last verse detracts from, if not ruins, the psalm's wide-eyed wonderment. But for the ancient listener, this imprecation against the wicked made perfect sense in a world that was otherwise perceived as harmoniously vibrant. By exhorting God to destroy the wicked in the final verse, the psalmist has decisively transferred the evil and chaos traditionally associated with mythically monstrous figures like Leviathan and placed them squarely on human shoulders. Conflict is most savage, most cruel, most wicked, among human beasts.

We don't know whom specifically the psalmist had in mind when he called God to consume the wicked. Were they foreigners, like the Babylonians, who destroyed much of his people's land and uprooted many from

7. Quoted in David Beerling, *The Emerald Planet: How Plants Changed Earth's History* (Oxford: Oxford University Press, 2007), vi.

8. Beerling, *The Emerald Planet,* vi.

their homes to eke out their survival elsewhere? Or were they internal to the community — kings who conscripted Israelite farmers into military service, taking from their families and their land? Whoever they were, they apparently posed a threat to creation's integrity. Positively, this grim conclusion rescues the psalm from viewing the world through rose-colored spectacles, from romanticizing reality. The psalmist acknowledges both predator and prey. Here is an authentic assessment of creation as it stands, not as it once was in some pristine state or as it will be in some future fulfillment. Here is a world in which the purveyors of chaos are not mythically monstrous — monsters made in the image of animals — but monstrously human.

Yes, the psalmist helps us to see the enemy in the mirror. No other species has changed the shape of the earth more than we have, and particularly within the last fifty years. Some scientists deem this new geological epoch ruled by humanity the "Anthropocene epoch," following the Pleistocene and the Holocene. The power that we wield today exceeds anything else on earth. And what are we doing with that power? We are destroying precisely those marvelous features of creation the psalmist commends to God's enjoyment: habitats and their inhabitants. We are systematically eliminating the very reasons for God to enjoy creation, and this is not God's will (cf. Rev. 11:18; see chapter 16). God's joy to the world is turning into God's despair of the world. The psalmist's "fanfare for the common creature" is failing because the orchestra is losing its members.

Care for other species as well as our own, the psalmist reminds us, is an exercise of joy. The psalm places God's joy squarely upon the shoulders of human responsibility. So Calvin may be right: "When God sees that the good things which he bestows are polluted by our corruptions, God ceases to take delight in bestowing them." "The stability of the world," Calvin concludes, "depends on this rejoicing of God in his works."[9] Sober words from a not so austere churchman, from Calvin the ecologist. The psalmist would agree. The creator's delight in serving creation requires reciprocal engagement on the part of the creature.

As wine "gladdens the human heart," so creation's wild and wooly variety gladdens God's heart. God savors it all not as creation's consumer but as its provider and sustainer. What, then, for those made in God's image? For the ancient psalmist, it is incumbent upon God's most powerful creatures to ensure that divine delight is sustained so that all the world be sustained. Now that would be a wonder.

---

9. Calvin, *Psalms*, 6.170.

7. *Wounded Wonder*

JOB 38–42

I have become a brother to jackals, and a companion to ostriches.

Job 30:29

To be the last man in the rhinoceros herd is, in fact, to be a monster.

Thomas Merton[1]

It is best at the outset to set aside a couple of popular misconceptions about the book of Job. One is that Job solves the problem of innocent suffering, what is commonly referred to as "theodicy." Not a bit. The book of Job is more about wonder than about suffering, less about theodicy and more about thaumaturgy, about mystery. Another misconception is that Job was a quintessentially patient man, despite the King James translation of James 5:11.[2] Job, as we shall see, is anything but the model of patience.

Job never receives an answer from God about his suffering. Instead, he gets from God a crushing dose of wonder, as Job's own words testify:

---

1. Commenting on Eugène Ionesco's play *Rhinoceros*. In Thomas Merton, *Raids on the Unspeakable* (New York: New Directions, 1964), 20.
2. "Endurance" or "perseverance" is a better translation of *hypomone*. Patience connotes quiet acceptance, which Job does not model.

> Therefore, I have declared what I did not discern,
> > things too wonderful for me, which I did not understand. (42:3b)

Uttered after his encounter with the voice "out of the whirlwind," Job's words testify to raw, unmitigated wonder. But what precisely did Job "discern"? What were those "things too wonderful" for Job? To answer these questions, we need to go back to the beginning of Job's riches-to-rags story and follow his journey from wound to wonder.

In the Beginning

Job's story begins in the "land of Uz," which could just as well be the land of Oz in light of its uncertain location (perhaps somewhere in northern Arabia). Regardless of his place of origin, what is important is that Job is not an Israelite. He is an Uzzite, and his outsider status allows him to pose unorthodox questions and make claims that challenge conventional ways of thinking about God. Yet Job is not a complete outlier. He is described as the perfect embodiment of righteousness: "Blameless and upright, one who feared God and avoided evil" (1:1). These are the stringent standards of religious piety, and Job excels at them all, so much so that he is considered "the greatest of all the people of the east" (1:3). Job is not an everyman, but he is the quintessentially serious man.

Job is also the quintessentially fallen man. His wealth drops off the fiscal cliff, and his reputation crumbles into notoriety and disgrace, all from God's doing. In the scene that unfolds beyond Job's perception, we find the divine assembly standing before the enthroned God of heaven. There, God questions "the satan,"[3] a heavenly being whose divinely appointed job is to roam the earth casting suspicion on seemingly righteous individuals, sort of like an aggressive district attorney in dogged pursuit of a case to prosecute. God boasts of Job: "Have you considered my servant Job? There is no one like him on the earth, a blameless and upright man who fears God and turns away from evil" (1:8). The satan remains unconvinced: "Does Job fear God for nothing?" (1:9). In other words: take away Job's

---

3. Not to be confused with Satan in the New Testament (e.g., Matt. 12:26; Luke 10:18; 22:3; Rom. 16:20). The figure of "the satan" in Job can also be found in 1 Chron. 21:1 and Zech. 3:1-2. The title (not a proper noun in the book of Job) means "adversary" or "inciter," as described above.

wealth and all other signs of blessing, and will Job remain righteous? Or will he curse God, now that his motivation for reverence has been taken away? Put another way: is Job righteous only by virtue of God's blessings, or is his righteousness righteous for its own sake, regardless of outcome or motivation?

The satan proposes a test that is found agreeable by God: Job is to be stripped of all his blessings, including his children and his health, to determine the true basis of his righteousness. And so God and the satan wait to see how Job reacts. Like God waiting to see how Adam responds to the animals in the garden, now God waits to see whether Job can persevere in righteousness amid such horrific suffering. Will Job curse God now that his own world has become accursed? Will he disparage the God who, unbeknownst to him, is testing him? Will Job step out of character as the world around him has been thrown off kilter? One can only wait and wonder. In the meantime, the book of Job begins with an unspeakable travesty: it is *because* of his righteousness that Job has unwittingly become the victim of an experiment in pain, whose outcome will be determined by what Job has to say to God and about God.

What possibly could be going on in God's mind to agree to such a test? Is God really not sure whether Job's righteousness is valid? Or is God absolutely sure but intends to prove a point against the satan at Job's expense? What would compel God's consent to allow the perpetration of misfortune against an innocent individual? The text does not come clean on God's motivation, nor perhaps is it able to, given the narrative constraints. Like a sordid tale from the Brothers Grimm, a folk story about a wager between God and the satan over a righteous individual sounds like a setup, leaving the reader to wrestle with its troubling implications. The prose tale of Job's troubles seems designed to provoke more questions than answers. In any event, God does not come off very well in the first two chapters (and most of the following chapters, for that matter). As the satan casts suspicion on Job's integrity, so the reader is forced to do so regarding God's.

In view of what the story both reveals and conceals, it is best to think of the book of Job as something of a thought experiment. Job revels in "what if?" questions about human integrity, divine intention, and even the nature of the universe, all crashing down upon the character of Job. *What if* the paragon of righteousness were to fall into unimaginable ruin and disgrace? *What if* piety were more than a matter of reward and blessing? *What if* righteousness invited vulnerability and suffering? *What if* God were no protector of the righteous? *What if* the world does not operate justly? From the Joban prologue to the climactic divine speeches to the "happy" epilogue, the book of Job is filled with "what if" wonderings.

Not coincidentally, most of the book consists of Job's responses to these questions, and he begins with simple, stoic acceptance: "Naked I came from my mother's womb, and naked I will return there; the LORD has given, and the LORD has taken away; blessed be the name of the LORD" (1:21); and: "Shall we receive the good from God and not receive the bad?" (2:10). From the narrator's prosaic perspective, Job proves himself righteous under the most trying of circumstances by accepting his misfortunes with utter deference toward God. No curse is found on his lips or under his breath. As the narrator declares, "In all this Job did not sin or charge God with wrongdoing" (1:22).

But things change dramatically as the story of Job changes hands from narrator to poet. Beginning in chapter 3, Job becomes the lament made flesh, the complainant par excellence. No longer the patriarch of patience, Job's emotionally charged, poetic words deconstruct the confident assessment of his impassive profile in the narrative prologue. Job is filled with angst and anger; he is determined to end his life by cursing the day of his birth — a variant of his wife's advice! — and in so doing dragging all of God's creation down with him. "Let that day be darkness!" Job cries out (3:4a), a stinging counterpoint to God's "Let there be light" (Gen. 1:3). Job's suicidal words verge on the ecocidal by linking the fate of creation to his own. The solace of chaos is what Job desires in the wake of his loss and suffering. His lament, and all that follows, begins to confirm the satan's charges. Indeed, the next step, and a very short step at that, would be for Job to curse God and die, just as his wife urged him to do. But, for better or worse, Job's friends interrupt his slide into oblivion, the comfort he seeks in death, by offering their "consolations."

Job's friends clearly never took Pastoral Counseling 101. Their words of "comfort" spark only angry debate. Where there should have been empathy, there is only outrage. Where there should have been outreach, we only find only entrenchment. Disputation replaces consolation. Job and his "friends" go around and around in their dialogical exchanges, getting nowhere. Job is no more comforted in his misery than his friends are convinced of his innocence. Although no resolution is reached in these dialogues (Job 3–27), we do see a remarkable transformation take place. Job's desire shifts from death-wish to self-vindication, or, if we go back to the narrative prologue (Job 1–2), from deference to defiance. Job presents a

73

monstrous anomaly to his friends: he is blameless yet, in light of his suffering, eminently blameworthy. The only way the "friends" can make sense of Job's plight is to impugn his character, to regard him as having committed some egregious act that would have warranted such suffering. Thus they seek to convince Job of his need to confess and repent so that God might restore him. Job, on the other hand, knows he's innocent and blames God for committing a miscarriage of justice. Job's grief has turned to grievance. He smells betrayal, both human and divine. He feels abandoned, forsaken by friend and God alike. He has nothing except chaos within and around him:

> My inward parts churn without relief;
>> days of misery overtake me.
> I wander about in sunless gloom;
>> I stand up in the assembly and cry out.
> I have become a brother to jackals,
>> and a companion to ostriches. (30:27-29)

The last verse is perhaps the most telling. Rejected by his community and what is left of his family, all Job has left are "jackals" and "ostriches" to keep him company. Of course, Job is speaking poetically and not without a touch of sarcasm: ostriches and jackals symbolize devastation. Such animals inhabit cities that lie in ruins, devoid of human population (Isa. 34:13). Job's life lies in shambles as unwelcomed visitors roam about at will.

Wild Wonder

Speaking of unwelcomed: God finally arrives upon the scene but not on particularly intimate terms. In a fierce whirlwind, God's presence inspires more terror than comfort (38:1). But because such terror turns out to be the medium of revelation, it is terror turned wondrous.[4] It is the voice, not the wind or the storm, that "smites" Job. Blow by blow, Job is struck not with bolts of lightning but with myriad questions and challenges: Who is this? Where were you? Can you? Have you? Where? Who? Yes, such questions aim to put Job in his place, to drive home his creaturely

---

4. Scott C. Jones, "Corporeal Discourse in the Book of Job," *Journal of Biblical Literature* 132 (2013): 845-63 at 854.

status. But at the same time they also serve to blow wide open his horizon of perception.[5]

To Job and his dark, morose world, fashioned by curse and death-wish (Job 3:3-9), God thunders out, "Lighten up!" Through the power of poetry, God casts the world, including Job's world, in a new light. God shows Job a world far beyond his ken: the earth's foundations, the swaddled sea, the gates of deep darkness, storehouses of hail, light's dwelling place, flowing channels in the desert — all beyond human reach and control. After describing the heights and depths of creation, God shows Job a host of wild animals: lion and raven, mountain goats and deer, wild ass and ox, ostrich and war horse, hawk and vulture, Behemoth and Leviathan, six pairs total. Each animal, God proudly points out, exhibits its own dignity and strength, its fearlessness and independence. They are not, it turns out, contemptible scavengers or purveyors of chaos but treasured creatures, each admired by God, each holding its rightful place in creation.

The world, as it turns out, is full of wild and brutal beauty. The wild ass roams the steppe far from the city, far from its domesticated cousin, the donkey. No beast of burden is the wild ox. The fearless warhorse charges into battle without a moment's hesitation, while the ostrich laughs at the warhorse and its rider. The brood of vultures spy out the dead and "suck up" the blood of the slain (39:30). Unlike Adam, to whom God brought the animals to be named in the garden (Gen. 2:19-20), Job is poetically transported from his own world into the wild, to where the wild things are, to learn their names and their habits. God does not ask Job to kill the lion, as if to test his physical prowess in the face of predatory danger. Instead, God challenges Job to imagine himself *providing* for the lion, as if to test his care and compassion (Job 38:39).[6] Such a challenge turns Job's "civilized" world upside down: in God's kingdom Job should aspire to be not the lion hunter, not even the lion tamer, but the lion's provider.

The final two creatures, Behemoth and Leviathan, verge on the mythically horrific; they are larger than life, much more than the hippo and the crocodile, respectively, that some scholars make them out to be. Monsters they are, and God cherishes them. They too are God's children, and so also Job. "Behold Behemoth," God declares, "the first of God's great

---

5. For further detail of the background, shape, and message of God's answer to Job, see William P. Brown, *The Seven Pillars of Creation: The Bible, Science, and the Ecology of Wonder* (New York: Oxford University Press, 2010), 116-40.

6. Compare 10:16, where Job complains that God has hunted him down "as a lion"!

acts" (40:19), made *"with"* Job (40:15). The preposition is the key; it is the "with" of shared identity. It is as if Job has found in this monster his long-lost twin! Somehow this utterly alien beast, a quintessential object of wonder, is related to Job. In Behemoth, Job sees something of himself. In Behemoth, Job has found his own connection to the wild.

All in all, God casts Job farther out than his ash heap could ever take him. It is as if God turns Job's ash heap into a magic carpet to carry him to the farthest reaches of creation. Job is not only cast out to the edge of his community; he is catapulted to the very margins of creation itself, where beauty and fear converge. Job now sees himself as the *cosmic* outcast, a stranger in a terribly strange land. But perception is relative, Job learns. What was considered marginal to Job is deemed central by God. The outer limits of Job's world have now come front and center. The "out there" is now right here, right in front of Job. As Job lamented his association with the jackals and the ostriches in 30:29, God shows him what good company he actually has out in the margins! With Behemoth specifically, Job discovers he is no alien after all. He is connected to the wild; indeed, he discovers himself to be a child of the wild. Out there Job has (re)discovered God's compassion for the world, extending to the very margins in Job's eyes. After Job professes his wonder before the God of the whirlwind (42:2-6), he is restored, vindicated before his "friends," who had taken up the adversary's cause by doing all they could to dismantle his integrity. And what is the first thing Job does? He prays for them.

But Job's "restoration" is no mere return to how things were. In a world full of risk and danger, Job is given the chance to start a new family. To do so, in fact, would have been a bold move for Job, a move born of grief and forged in courage. Job painfully knows that there are no guarantees in this life. If anything, the book of Job is harsh testimony to this fact. But Job raises a new family anyway: ten children, same number of sons and daughters. This time, however, his daughters are given special names in the narrative, terms of endearment describing their exquisite beauty, and Job does something remarkably unpatriarchal with them: he gives them a share of his property that would have typically gone only to his sons, an unprecedented move in biblical tradition (cf. Num. 27 and 36). As Job's anguished words with his friends broke theological convention, so now his actions break social convention, upending traditional family values by dispensing material equality to his daughters. In so doing, Job grants his daughters a measure of autonomy in a world steeped in social dependency. It seems that Job has brought something of the wild back home. Although his place is not in the wild, Job lives with the wild in his heart. In God's final answer to Job, on God's cosmic tour of creation, Job's mind has become rewired and his heart "re-wilded." Were Job to write a self-help book in view of all that he has witnessed in wonder, he might title it *The Beauty of My Inner Beast.*

There and Back Again

Mary-Jane Rubenstein talks of the double movement of wonder, which "takes us out of the world only to put us back into the world, dismantling old possibilities to uncover new ones."[7] So, in fact, was Job's journey from wound to wonder: Job is cast out into the edge of community and creation to discover anew his identity as a child of God. He has come face to face with the God of the wild who attends to the outcast and the rejected, the untamable and the fierce, the ugly and the beautiful, the wild and the strange. And Job has found in them, in these denizens of the margins, God's care for him as well. No beasts of burden are to be found in God's wild kingdom, Job included. The God of the final answer, it turns out, is far different from the god of the initial wager. If Job has proved himself to be a different man from the one portrayed in the prose prologue, so God has proved to be a different deity.

God has found a place for Job in the wild, not for Job to live out in the wilderness but for Job to make a place for the wild back home. He comes back transformed, a bit of a wild man himself. Job has experienced "things too wonderful" out there and returns to discover the wonder of his own household, particularly that of his three daughters, whose beauty is commemorated by the names they are given. Job has come back awe-struck and freed. Having encountered firsthand the God of the wild, Job is released from the prison house of moralism and patriarchal convention, freed from the shackles of honor and shame, freed from himself as profiled in the prologue. He is an outsider who returns to be an insider transformed and ready to transform.

So how does Job spend the next 140 years of his life before he dies, "old and full of days" (42:17)? What does he do for "his children, and his children's children"? Who exactly has Job become? One can only wonder.

---

7. Mary-Jane Rubenstein, *Strange Wonder: The Closure of Metaphysics and the Opening of Awe,* Insurrections: Critical Studies in Religion, Politics, and Culture (New York: Columbia University Press, 2008), 60.

Into the Wild: An Addendum

Some of the wild animals described in Job 38–39 may seem a bit too tame and familiar for those raised on National Geographic or Animal Planet or the San Diego Zoo. There are other creatures, countless creatures in fact, that could easily be included in God's litany of wildness. Deep sea creatures, for example, which transgress the boundary between the beautiful and the grotesque.[8] Or desert creatures. I recently asked members of a class that took place in the high desert of New Mexico (Ghost Ranch) to supplement God's animals in the biblical book of Job with desert critters. And this is what they came up with:[9]

> Behold, Job, the **Gila monster**, which I made with you, the first of my great acts! Examine the beauty of its beaded gown. It lives in extreme conditions without water, waiting patiently for its prey. Do you know how long the mother waits for her eggs to hatch and how far under the earth she buries them? It survives on only six meals . . . *a year!* The male sniffs out its potential mate with the flick of its tongue and pleasures her unabated for two and a half hours! Come now, Job, see if you can do that!

> Look, Job, at the majestic flight of the **turkey vulture**, soaring in spirals on thermal updrafts. I delight in its menacing stare. See how it gazes down upon you, anticipating your death, eager to pick your bones, cleansing the land of your carcass and turning your rotting flesh into pure vitality. Job, can you turn death into life?

> *Voila,* the **diamondback rattlesnake**! Have you considered the strength and grace of its glide? Can you move with speed without the use of legs and strike within the twinkling of an eye? Can you grow a louder, longer rattle each year? Can you renew yourself each year with a new skin? And can you display great beauty and yet instill great terror in those who do not respect you? Job, feed what the diamondback desires!

8. See Brown, *Seven Pillars of Creation,* 138–40.

9. Many thanks to the sixty plus participants in the class "Desert Faith in a Desert Time," which took place June 24-29, 2013, at Ghost Ranch, New Mexico, along with Larry Rasmussen, Talitha Arnold, and Terry Tempest Williams.

Consider, Job, the *coyote*, a most clever creature in my wild kingdom. I rejoice in the various ways she adapts to almost any environment, from scorching deserts to hostile urban neighborhoods. She teaches her pups to stay with her as she slinks through the desert and disappears as a ghost. The coyote trots tirelessly, searching for sustenance wherever she can get it. The coyote is my ultimate survivalist (next to the cockroach).

Job, did you create the *black bear* to make her home in the glaciers and the desert? Did you create her to know the rhythms of activity and rest as she stores up fat to nourish herself in the deep sleep of hibernation? Did you wrap her in her glossy coat, protecting her from cold and heat as she moves through the harsh elements? Can you provide for the black bear and her cubs?

Behold, Job, the *scorpion*! Can you blend in with your surroundings, hidden and lying in wait to surprise and poison creatures of all kinds? Can you strike fear in the hearts of beasts a thousand times your size with the speed and sting of your barbed tail?

Who gives the *bighorn sheep* the agility to scale sheer cliffs? Who made the wild bighorn so majestic with its crown of horns? Who made the sheep so capable of going without water for so long, with freedom to roam the desert? Who made the bighorn so well clothed for the harsh elements, adapting to extreme heat and cold? Look, Job, at how brave the bighorn is before the heights and sheer cliffs!

Have you felt the rough and intricate shell of the *desert tortoise* as she draws inward to protect her core? Do you know the secret that prolongs her life and the wisdom that she has to spend the day with such slow pace and patience?

Look, Job, there's the *mountain lion*! How great is the power of her back legs and how wonderful is the way she uses her magnificent tail for balance. Have you noticed how she gently protects and nurses her young? Observe how she roams great distances and protects her boundaries. Observe her nocturnal abilities: her eyes and sensitive whiskers can detect the slightest movement in the darkness. She generously leaves portions of her kill to other animals for their survival.

Job, can you weave a garment of silk as beautiful as the ***tarantula*** and make it useful? Do you possess the wisdom to know just when to strike and when to leave things alone? Can you give birth to a thousand babies and tenderly teach them all they need to know for life in six days before they disperse to live on their own, never to return?

And Job said, "I have declared what I did not discern, things too wonderful for me, which I did not understand."

8. *Mundane Wonder*

ECCLESIASTES

There is nothing better for someone than to eat and drink,
and find enjoyment in one's toil.

Ecclesiastes 2:24

Ecclesiastes has been called the strangest book in the Bible, and for good reason. Some consider it a book of deep despair and pessimism; others, a meditation on joy. Some regard the book as the scattered musings of a confused sage. Others find profound lessons about life. Given such divided readings, perhaps all that can be said with certainty is that Ecclesiastes is the Bible's most *enigmatic* book. Replete with contradictions, paradoxes, and ambiguities, Ecclesiastes inspires nothing short of bewildered curiosity. The book is a puzzle, for the most part an unsolvable one. Yet for all its baffling qualities and interpretive challenges, Ecclesiastes bears a remarkably universal appeal. It bears an uncanny ability to speak to a wide range of readers across generations, cultures, and contexts. Such is the book's wonder, its genius in fact. Ecclesiastes is a book for all seasons.

The main character of Ecclesiastes calls himself Qoheleth (New Revised Standard Version: "the Teacher"), but his historical identity remains shrouded in mystery. His allegedly royal pedigree ("son of David") quickly fades away after the first two chapters. *Qoheleth* in Hebrew means something like "assembler." But here, too, there is ambiguity. In context, the verbal root can mean one of two things, or perhaps both: *convene* an assembly consisting, perhaps, of students, or *collect* things such as wisdom sayings and instructions (7:27). Both roles suit Qoheleth well. As an auditor, Qoheleth takes an inventory of life by collecting and codifying the "data" of experience, both individual (his own) and collective (tradition). As a teacher, Qoheleth candidly shares the results of his work to his gathered audience, both ancient and modern.

Royal Pain

Qoheleth introduces himself not until 1:12, where he describes himself as "king over Israel in Jerusalem." The title of the book (1:1) adds a further detail: "the son of David." This would cast Qoheleth in the guise of King Solomon, even though the book itself, given its language and content, reflects a much later time, specifically the Hellenistic period, sometime after 333 B.C.E. (The historical Solomon lived some six centuries earlier.)

The irony of such self-identification is that Qoheleth dons Solomon's regal robe only to take it off. As "king," Qoheleth conducts an experiment of sorts. He intends to investigate everything by means of wisdom, through observation and scrutiny, in order to find, ultimately, some insight into God's purposes in the world. As "king," Qoheleth has all the means at his disposal to conduct such an investigation: wisdom, power, resources, and an insatiable curiosity. Qoheleth fully embodies the saying in Proverbs 25:2: "It is the glory of God to conceal things, but the glory of kings is to search things out." Qoheleth casts himself as the world's quintessential "seeker." And with his Solomonic conceit, Qoheleth boasts of his royal wherewithal "to search things out" without limitation. And so the sage begins by investigating "pleasure" in order to find out what is ultimately "good for mortals" (Eccles. 2:1-3). He builds monuments, amasses vast possessions, including slaves and concubines, and explores "the delights of the flesh" (2:4-8). No desire is left unfulfilled (2:10). The outcome? Utter disappointment: "Then I considered all that my hands had done and the toil I had spent in doing it, and again, all was futility and a chasing after wind, and there was nothing to be gained under the sun" (2:11). The royal experiment has failed.

Related to his royal image, Qoheleth presents himself as the consummate examiner of life, the Bible's first and only philosopher. Like Socrates, he is driven by the conviction that "the unexamined life is not worth living." With the best of credentials and the greatest of expectations, the sage embarks on his heroic quest for the meaning of life. But he comes back empty handed. Like Saul Bellow, this sage attaches an addendum to the Socratic motto: "But the examined life makes you wish you were dead."[1]

Cosmic Futility

Qoheleth's royal failure is read into reality itself. For whatever reason, the sage's opening words are not autobiographical but cosmological in nature, prompted by his leading question concerning toil and gain (1:3). This opening question strikes at the heart of human purpose. "Gain" *(yitron)* is more than "a penny saved, a penny earned." Rather, it is whatever ensures one's legacy for posterity. Toil is the effort exerted for gainful living, and questioning its value, in turn, places all creation in question. In the sage's eyes, creation itself has a cosmic stake in the pursuit of gain, and Qoheleth, in turn, has a personal stake in creation's purpose.

Generations come and go, the sun rises and sets, the wind blows hither and yon, and the streams flow perpetually, all the while both earth and sea remain unchanged. The sage observes the weary "revolutions" of the sun, whose "panting" to the place of its rising is matched by the wind's unceasing circumambulations. Sun, wind, and streams are all in constant motion, all returning to where they began and, without pause, continuing on. The perpetual cycles exhibit neither beginning nor ending.

There is certainly wonder in the way creation (re)cycles itself, sustaining itself, but Qoheleth doesn't acknowledge it. For him, all the constant motion and effort that drives the cosmos yields nothing: *no* change, *no* gain. Even as the millennia pass, any semblance of progress, any appearance of newness is merely a mirage: "There is nothing new under the sun" (1:9). Activity abounds, but nothing is achieved. Like a hamster spinning its wheel, no destination is reached. Such frenetic motion amounts to only running in place. All this cosmic kinesis is for naught. Ever in motion but never changing, the cosmos is uniformly indifferent to human living and aspiration, from birth to death, a world without pause and effect.

---

1. See Eccles. 4:2-3; 6:3 (but cf. 9:4). Quoted in Mel Gussow, "For Saul Bellow, Seeing the Earth with Fresh Eyes," *New York Times* (26 May 1997); accessed 17 September 2012 at http://www.nytimes.com/1997/05/26/books/for-saul-bellow-seeing-the-earth-with-fresh -eyes.html?scp=1&sq=Gussow%20%22Seeing%20the%20Earth%22&st=cse.

Beautiful Futility

Matching Qoheleth's opening poem on cosmic futility is his most well-known passage on life's "seasons." What Qoheleth does visually with his cosmic "snapshot" in 1:4-7, he now does temporally in 3:1-8. Both poetic reflections take a step back and look at the larger picture, the former cosmologically and the latter chronologically. If the life of the cosmos runs like a spinning wheel going nowhere, human life in Ecclesiastes 3 resembles something of a pendulum, swinging back and forth, swinging between opposite extremes. There are fourteen paired opposites featured, and being divisible by seven, this poetic catalogue conveys a sense of completion:

> For everything there is a season,
>> and a time for every matter under the heavens:
> a time to bear and a time to die;
>> a time to plant and a time to uproot what is planted;
> a time to kill and a time to heal;
>> a time to break and a time to build;
> a time to weep and a time to laugh;
>> a time to mourn and a time to dance;
> a time to throw stones and a time to gather stones;
>> a time to embrace and a time to refrain from embracing;
> a time to seek and a time to lose;
>> a time to keep and a time to throw away;
> a time to tear and a time to sew;
>> a time to be silent and a time to speak;
> a time to love and a time to hate;
>> a time of war and a time of peace.

There is something mesmerizing about this poem. Reading it is like listening to the hypnotic tick-tock of a grandfather clock. In his commentary on the poem, Qoheleth remarks: God "has made everything beautiful for its time" (3:11). This is the "beauty" of something eminently suitable for its time and context. Everything, both good and bad, finds its place within a divinely governed seasonal symmetry. These balanced polarities of human activity provoke nothing less than wonder for the sage who claims to have seen it all. Qoheleth uses the adjective "beautiful" (Hebrew *yapheh*) only one other time, as we shall see. But here such "beauty" reflects the seemingly perfect balance between laughter and mourning, love and hate, war and peace, all set within life's oscillations between life and death (also 1:4). Nevertheless, this elegant symmetry is no cause for celebration: life swings back and forth, never stationary but never going anywhere either. The incessant "swings" of human activity within time's disparities match the perpetual "cycles" of cosmic conduct. And so life oscillates indifferently between gain and loss, between prosperity and adversity. It is important to note that Qoheleth is trying to be dispassionately descriptive; he is not assigning equal value to war and peace, hate and love. It's just the way it is, he observes. It's just the way human beings act, for better *and* worse, for woe and for weal. The lesson? "In the day of prosperity rejoice, and in the day of adversity take care. God has made the one as well as the other, so that humans may not discern anything that will come after them" (7:14).

Qoheleth offers this "beautiful" poem as an invitation for wondering. Although complete in its own right with its balanced range of opposites, the poem invites the reader to supplement the sage's list of time's disparities. For example:

> A time to care for one's children;
>> a time to be cared for by one's children;
> a time to win and a time to lose;
>> a time to be sick and a time to feel vigorous;
> a time to give and a time to receive;
>> a time to render praise and a time to offer critique.

One could go on. Moreover, as our world becomes ever more interconnected due to the wonders of communication technology, we now know more than ever before that such "times," disparate that they are, can occur at the *same* time and virtually in the same place. In other words, we can easily translate Qoheleth's ancient poem from "time" to "place":

> For everything there is a place,
>> and a location for every matter under heaven:
> a place of affluence and a place of poverty;
>> a place of obesity and a place of malnutrition;
> a place flooding and a place of drought;
>> a place of famine and a place of plenty;
> a place of storm and a place of calm;
>> a place of freedom and a place of bondage.

One could go on. Qoheleth concludes his poem by raising the same question posed at the beginning of his cosmic poem (3:9; 1:3): what gain is there in all the toiling, in all the activity? Nothing, the sage claims. Or put it this way: what do you get when you work your fingers to the bone? Bony fingers.

Qoheleth's verdict on all that he has seen and witnessed is "vanity" (1:2; 12:8). "Vanity" *(hevel)* is the book's single-word thesis. The sage presents one example after another of life's *hevel,* from the cosmic to the personal. Frequently paired with the expression "chasing wind," the word itself conjures the image of "vapor," something ephemeral and insubstantial, perhaps even noxious. Nevertheless, *hevel* bears a host of nuances in Qoheleth's discourse. The term can be translated in a number of related ways: futility, absurdity, nothingness, worthlessness, transience, ephemerality, delusion, insignificance, and shit all have been proposed, and no doubt a measure of translational flexibility is needed in each place where it is found in Qoheleth's musings. But regardless of its specific nuance within a specific context, it is clear for Qoheleth that "*hevel* happens" (a good bumper sticker!), and death is the stellar instance of *hevel* happening. Put cosmically, *hevel* robs the world of meaningful coherence. Put personally, *hevel* drives a wedge between one's action and expected outcome. In either case, *hevel* is the harbinger of systemic failure.

Failure it is for the entire world. If the world in Ecclesiastes 1 is a cosmos running in perpetuity, then the world according to Ecclesiastes 12 is a cosmos running on empty. As generations come and go (1:5), so all creation will eventually go (away). For Qoheleth, creation may not have had a beginning, but it surely has an ending. The end marks a return to creation's preexistent state before the *adam* was created from "dust" and infused with God's breath (Gen. 2:7). Between darkness and dust, the sage employs a variety of images ranging from the domestic and the commercial to the natural and the cosmic, all to demonstrate how death affects all areas of life. The sun "panting" in Ecclesiastes 1:5 suffers burnout in 12:2. The toiling self of 4:8 is dead and buried in 12:5-7. The world's end is no apocalyptic overthrow. Rather, it happens with gradual darkening and diminution. The perpetual cycles and swings of creation's regularities simply unwind. The world passes away in cosmic dissolution and bodily deterioration. Call it entropy . . . or *hevel.*

Feasting on Wonder

But even in a life fraught with "vanity" or futility and ultimately death, the sage does not recommend despair, even though his words smack of melancholy. As a way of life in the face of *hevel*, Qoheleth commends enjoyment, specifically enjoyment manifest in eating, drinking, and finding pleasure in one's work. This, in fact, is the second matter the ancient sage finds "beautiful" (*yapheh;* 5:18; cf. 3:11). Qoheleth's commendation of enjoyment is given seven times throughout his discourse (2:24-26; 3:12-13; 3:22; 5:18-20; 8:15; 9:7-9; 11:7-10). Here are two of his commendations:

> There is nothing better for someone than to eat and drink and find enjoyment in toil. This also, I saw, is from the hand of God. (2:24)

> This is what I have seen to be good: it is beautiful [*yapheh*] to eat and drink and find enjoyment in all the toil with which one toils under the sun the few days of life that God has given, for that is one's portion. (5:18)

In the second commendation, the adjective "beautiful," as in 3:11, conveys a sense of wondrous suitability or fittingness. In 3:11, Qoheleth observed the elegance of perfectly paired opposites covering the range of human activity all nested in God's inscrutable providence. Here, the sage narrows his sights considerably to focus on the simple pleasures of eating, drinking, and finding some enjoyment in work.

The last two commendations in Ecclesiastes are more extensive and detailed. Qoheleth's language, moreover, has shifted from simple observation to urgent directive:

> Go, eat your bread with enjoyment, and drink your wine with a cheerful heart; for God has already approved what you do. Let your garments always be white; do not let oil be lacking on your head. Enjoy life with the woman you love, all the days of your fleeting [*hevel*] life, all your fleeting days that [God] has given you under the sun, because that is your portion in life and in your toil at which you toil under the sun. (9:7-9)

> Light is sweet, and it is pleasant for the eyes to see the sun. Even if one should live many years, let him rejoice in them all and remember that

the days of darkness may be many. All that comes is fleeting [*hevel*]. Rejoice, young man, while you remain young, and let your heart delight you in the days of your youth. Follow the ways of your heart and whatever your eyes see, and know that for all these things God will bring you into judgment. Banish anxiety from your heart, and remove pain from your body; for youth and the dawn of life are fleeting. (11:7-10)

Taken together, these various commendations view enjoyment as both a divine gift and a human duty. On the one hand, it is God's gift to human beings, whose lives are brief and whose ignorance of the future is pervasive. Enjoyment, Qoheleth observes, has a mysteriously incidental quality to it. It is not an object of striving. Thus, when and to whom the refreshing breezes of delight blow, no human being can determine: all the more reason to relish enjoyment when it is received. On the other hand, enjoyment is also a matter of duty. Qoheleth's last two commendations are, in fact, commands. In the final one, the sage counsels a young man to fulfill his deepest desire with the warning that God will bring him into judgment for *failing* to do so (11:9)! Yes, Qoheleth's warning about divine judgment is not to repress the young man but to release and encourage him to find suitable objects of desire. It is a "kick-in-the-pants" kind of warning, not a cower-in-fear kind of judgment. Divine judgment is intended to reinforce the exhortation to "follow the ways of your heart," not to impede it.[2]

For Qoheleth, enjoyment is a serendipity and a duty. It is a wonder, a paradox in which the human encounters the divine in mysterious interaction, a testament to both the "hand of God" and the human will. No fireworks or earth-shattering displays of glory here. A good meal, table fellowship, a marital moment, meaningful work — all are "mundane wonders," wonders that lack the sense of the sensational but are just as fulfilling and uplifting as any wonder could be, the kind of wonder that brings a tear of joy or a simple smile, even if it doesn't quite take your breath away. To welcome mundane wonder also counters a world that is hell-bent on striving for gain *ad infinitum*, a world obsessed with the sensational and the self-enriching. To an obsessive world the sage offers subversive advice.[3] This,

2. For further argumentation along this line, see W. Sibley Towner, "Ecclesiastes," in *New Interpreter's Bible*, ed. Leander Keck and Richard Clifford (Nashville: Abingdon, 1997), 5.265-360 at 353; and Thomas Krüger, *Qoheleth: A Commentary*, trans. O. C. Dean Jr., ed. K. Baltzer, Hermeneia (Minneapolis: Fortress, 2004), 196-97.

3. See Ralph C. Griffin III, "The Subversive Sage: Qoheleth and the Praxis of Resistance," Th.M. thesis (Decatur, GA: Columbia Theological Seminary, 2014).

at last, is Qoheleth's momentous discovery, made only after his supremely royal failure. It is the simple wonder of food, provided by God, shared at table, and enjoyed in fellowship. "Feasting" on wonder is the small but crucial success behind the sage's "failed" experiment in living. Mundane as it may be, the occasion "to eat and drink" is nothing less than a matter of supreme joy. It is the ecstasy of simplicity that Qoheleth has found. But what Qoheleth may not have fully realized is that to welcome such joy and to savor it, to cultivate and embody it, can indeed change the world. And that would be something new under the sun.

9. *Erotic Wonder*

SONG OF SONGS

Love is as fierce as death, passion as severe as Sheol;
   its flames are fiery flames, a raging flame.

Song of Songs 8:6b

While Qoheleth commends following one's desire (Eccles. 11:9), the Song of Songs aims to arouse desire, specifically erotic desire. It may come as a surprise, delightful or shocking, to know that the Bible contains a robust body of love poetry, a collection that could be called "Fifty Shades of Green."[1] Indeed, the Song's preferred setting for lovemaking, whether figurative or literal, is a lush garden . . . and a "green" couch (1:16).

The power of the Bible's love poetry derives first and foremost from the entwined dialogue of two embodied voices.[2] Although the woman and the man remain nameless, we come to know them as lovers in a relationship of mutual infatuation. At times they intermingle in

---

1. A play on the title of the 2012 bestseller *Fifty Shades of Grey* by E. L. James (New York: Vintage, 2012). Lest the reader take offense at what is intended to be a playful allusion, let me simply point out that the color makes all the difference! Green is for sustainable, mutually edifying love, not S&M.

2. It is worth nothing that the feminine voice dominates the collection: 53 percent of the text is spoken by females and 34 percent by males; Carol Meyers, "'To Her Mother's House': Considering a Counterpart to the Israelite *Bêt 'āb*," in *Bible and the Politics of Exegesis: Essays in Honor of Norman K. Gottwald on His Sixty-Fifth Birthday*, ed. David Jobling et al. (Cleveland: Pilgrim, 1991), 39-51 at 45.

conversation (e.g., 1:9-2:7; 4:1–5:1); at other times they speak separately about each other and to each other (3:1-5, 6-11; 7:1-9). Each addresses the other in praise of his or her desirability, physical and emotional. Each woos the other to join in lovemaking. Each is claimed for the other: "My beloved is mine, and I am his" (2:16); "I am my beloved's, and my beloved is mine" (6:3). In short, each is captivated by the erotic wonder of the other; each is awestruck, even lovesick, over the other.[3] From start to finish, their discourse is charged with mutual admiration and arousal. Desire is heightened by the seductive poetry, but it is also checked on occasion. Three times the woman declares to her female companions, "I charge you, O daughters of Jerusalem . . . do not arouse or awaken love until it is ready," that is, until the time is right (2:7; 3:5; 8:4). No wonder this admonition is given precisely when the poetry is about to burst (2:6; 3:4; 8:3).

To explore the Song's erotic wonder, it may suffice simply to let the poetry speak for itself, without commentary. But a biblical scholar cannot resist adding a few words, and for good reasons. Some of the alluring imagery featured in the poetry will likely sound strange to modern ears, and so some unpacking is necessary. Moreover, in English translations it is difficult to identify who's speaking. The following discussion thus aims to orient the reader to the Song's poetic beauty and to heighten his or her appreciation of its erotic awe. The Song of Songs excels in the art of arousal without being pornographic in so far that the objects of affection are compelling subjects of emotional depth and exquisite expression. They are sexual subjects in their own right, and the reader is invited to admire and celebrate their love for each other. Rather than a voyeur privy to the sexual fantasies of two lovers from afar, the reader is invited to be part of a dialogical *ménage à trois* of lyrical lovemaking.[4]

In Praise of Bodies

The praise one has for the other is unabashedly physical. Both lovers express their admiration for the other's body with metaphorical flair. The

---

3. While both are awestruck over each other, it is the woman who expresses her lovesickness, particularly with regard to the man's absence (2:5; 5:8).

4. This is discussed with greater nuance by J. Cheryl Exum, *Song of Songs*, Old Testament Library (Louisville: Westminster John Knox, 2005), 7-9.

man, for example, praises the woman's beauty body part by body part, from eyes to breasts:

> How beautiful you are, my friend,
> > how beautiful!
> Your eyes are doves behind your veil.
> > Your hair is like a flock of goats, winding down[5] Mount Gilead.
> Your teeth are like a flock of shorn ewes coming up from the wash,
> > all of them bearing twins, without miscarriage.
> Your lips are like a scarlet thread; your mouth is lovely.
> > Your cheek(?)[6] behind your veil is like a slice of pomegranate.
> Your neck is like the tower of David, built in courses;
> > on it hang a thousand shields, all of them warriors' bucklers.
> Your breasts are like two fawns, twins of a gazelle,
> > grazing among the lilies. (4:1-5)

Striking is the sheer diversity of images drawn from horticultural, pastoral, military, and wilderness settings. Together they form an impression of graceful elegance and formidable strength. The woman reciprocates as she describes her lover:

> My beloved is radiant and ruddy,
> > foremost among ten thousand.
> His head is finest gold;
> > his locks are curly(?),[7] dark as a raven.
> His eyes are like doves beside ravines of water,
> > bathed in milk, set by brimming pools.
> His cheeks are like beds of spices, pouring forth perfume.
> > His lips are lilies, dripping flowing myrrh.
> His arms are golden rods, studded with jewels.
> > His body is an ivory plate(?), encrusted with sapphires.
> His legs are marble columns, set upon golden pedestals.
> > His appearance is like Lebanon, choice as the cedars. (5:10-15)

5. The verb is rare. See Steven S. Tuell, "A Riddle Resolved by an Enigma: Hebrew *glš* and Ugaritic GLT," *Journal of Biblical Literature* 112 (1993): 99-104; and Exum, *Song of Songs*, 153.

6. The meaning is much debated. The term could also mean brow or temple.

7. Debated meaning, since the term occurs only here in the Hebrew Bible. See discussion in Marvin H. Pope, *Song of Songs: A New Translation with Introduction and Commentary,* Anchor Bible 7C (Garden City, NY: Doubleday, 1977), 536.

The woman casts the man with images that range from delicate to solid: tender doves and marble pillars, wavy locks and majestic cedars. Sturdiness and tenderness are wedded together in the woman's praise of the man.

Not to be bested, the man offers the most elaborate poetic praise of his beloved, from feet to face:

> How graceful are your sandaled feet, O noble woman!
>> Your curvaceous thighs are like jewels, the handiwork of an
>>> artisan.
> Your navel is a rounded goblet never lacking in mixed wine.
>> Your belly is a heap of wheat encircled with lilies.
> Your breasts are like two fawns, twins of a gazelle.
>> Your neck is like an ivory tower.
> Your eyes are pools in Heshbon by the gate of Bath-rabbim.
>> Your nose is like a tower of Lebanon keeping watch over
>>> Damascus.
> Your head is like Mount Carmel upon you,
>> the locks of your head are like purple (tapestry);
>>> a king is held captive in the tresses.
> How beautiful, how exquisite you are, O love, with your delights!
>> You are as stately as the palm tree; your breasts are like its
>>> clusters.
> I say, I shall climb the palm tree and grasp its branches.
>> May your breasts be like clusters of grape,
>>> and the scent of your breath like apples,
> and your mouth like choicest wine flowing smoothly for lovers,[8]
>> gliding over lips and teeth. (7:1-9)

From bottom to top, the man lingers lovingly under and around the woman. He is held captive by every part of her body (nose included), and then climactically likens her to a "palm tree" for climbing as he reaches her breasts and mouth. As the poetry proceeds, the man rises up until he stands erect to embrace his partner.

Both the man and the woman deploy a host of similes and metaphors to describe each other's body. Such imagery, of course, cannot be taken literally with anatomical precision. The images are evocatively

---

8. See the discussion of this disputed term in Exum, *Song of Songs,* 239.

metaphorical. To paint an actual portrait of the woman, for example, with such images (e.g., her neck and nose as towers) would amount to a grotesque figuration. No, the power of metaphor lies in its capacity to suggest, not dictate, and to reveal, not explain. The world of metaphor conjured in the text is a world the man and woman know quite intimately. Young gazelles and grape clusters remind the man of the woman's breasts; marble pillars evoke for the woman her lover's legs. Their shared wonder in each other's body, in turn, shapes how they see the world around them, whose enchantments serve as intimations of the other, signs of their deep desire for each other. As they gaze longingly at each other, they also turn outward to regard the world, pastoral and urban, wild and cultivated, from the perspective of their bodies. Indeed, they see the world through their bodies, and the world, consequently, is made exquisite by their mutual affections. Through their love for each other, the world itself becomes enchanted.

To the man, the woman exudes a beauty that proves irresistible. Twice she is described as formidably lovely, both by the man and by her maidens:

> You are beautiful as Tirzah, my friend, lovely as Jerusalem,
>   terrible [*ayom*] as bannered armies. (6:4)

> Who is this that looks down like the dawn,
>   beautiful as the moon, radiant as the sun,
>   terrible [*ayummah*] as bannered armies? (6:10)

Beauty and terror are conjoined poetically in these verses, and they converge bodily in the woman. A terrible beauty she is. The man even pleads at one point: "Avert your eyes from me; they overwhelm me!" (6:5). Resistance proves futile. Fair as she is formidable, the woman inspires a fearful wonder. The man is awestruck: "You have ravished my heart,[9] my sister, my bride, you have ravished my heart with one glance of your eyes, with one jewel of your necklace" (4:9). Is this complaint or praise, fear or joy, coming from the man? Does he want to take flight or surrender? Or both? In any event, a mere glance is all it takes, and the man is smitten, pierced to the heart, as good as dead. The woman is a dreadful delight, an awful beauty. She is a thing of wonder.

9. The verb translated as "ravish" *(lbb)* comes from the word "heart."

Journeys of Desire

The poetry of love alternates between description and invitation, between admiration and action. The man beckons the woman to depart with him, now that the time is ripe for love:

> My beloved speaks and says to me:
>   "Arise, my love, my friend, and come away;
> for, behold, the winter is past,
>   the rains are over and gone." (2:10-11; cf. 4:8)

The woman issues her own invitation:

> Come, my beloved, let us go out into the fields,
>   and lodge in the villages;
> let us go early to the vineyards;
>   let us see if the vines have blossomed,
> and the grape blossoms have opened
>   and the pomegranates have bloomed.
> There I will give my love to you. (7:11-12)

The scene is hauntingly beautiful: the woman imagines herself and her beloved going out before sunrise to delight in the first signs of new life out in the cultivated fields. The budded vines and opened blossoms welcome the couple's lovemaking. The woman's invitation is climactic: now, finally, is the time for love to be awakened, for passion to be aroused (cf. 2:7; 3:5; 8:4). In her invitation, the woman opens herself to the man beside the blooming pomegranate trees.

In a very different scene, the woman lies in bed at night, awake and yearning for her lover:

> I slept, but my heart was alert.
>   Listen! My beloved is knocking.
> "Open to me, my sister, my friend, my dove, my perfect one;
>   for my head is drenched with dew, my locks with the drops of the
>   night."
> I had stripped off my robe. Must I put it on again?
>   I had washed my feet. Must I get them dirty?
> My beloved reached his hand into the opening,

and my body stirred because of him.
I arose to open to my beloved, my hands dripping with myrrh,
my fingers with liquid myrrh, upon the handles of the bolt.

(5:2-5)

In this night dream sequence, the man beseeches the woman to "open" to him, and she consents, but not without hesitation. The man's action with his hand anticipates intercourse in his attempt to open the locked door (cf. 4:12), which arouses the woman (literally, her "bowels stirred for him"). As she arises to open, she is dripping, her fragrant fingers ready to grasp his hand. But she discovers that her lover has vanished:

I opened to my beloved,
    but my beloved had turned and was gone!
I swooned because of him.[10]
    I sought him, but could not find him;
I called him,
    but he gave no answer. (5:6)

The woman is left only with unfulfilled desire, and so she wanders the city in search:

The watchmen found me as they patrolled the city;
    they struck me and bruised me,
        they took my mantle from me, those watchmen of the walls.
I charge you, O daughters of Jerusalem, if you find my beloved,
    tell him this: I am lovesick. (5:7-8)

Wandering at night in search for love typically brings danger rather than discovery, abuse rather than fulfillment. We are not told why the watchmen beat her. Some conjecture that they mistook her for a prostitute, but the text does not clarify. Perhaps the point is this: desire possesses her and presses her onward, despite the dangers. She is not deterred from seeking her lover in the dark of night in the city, where danger lurks. Her torment vividly illustrates the perils of love, the lengths to which a lover will venture forth to seek and to find, even to the point of self-endangerment. Indeed, the woman proclaims twice how she is "lovesick" (*cholet ahabah;*

---

10. Slight emendation of the vowel pointing is needed. See Exum, *Song of Songs,* 185.

1:5; 5:8). Love can be a terminal disease with only one cure: (re)u.
with the other.

A similar nocturnal sojourn takes place two chapters earlier, but thi.
time with a much happier outcome:

> On my bed at night I sought the one I love;
>> I sought him but found him not; I called him, but he gave no
>> answer.
> "I will rise now and roam the city, through the streets and the
>> squares;
> I will seek the one I love."
>> I sought him but found him not.
> The watchmen found me as they patrolled the city.
> "Have you seen the one I love?"
> Scarcely had I passed them when I found the one I love.
> I held him fast, and would not let him go,
>> until I brought him into my mother's house,
>>> and into the chamber of the one who conceived me.   (3:1-4)

Ironically resonant of the "strange" woman's pursuit of the young man
in Proverbs (Prov. 7:4-27), the lover in the Song finds and captures her
beloved and brings him home with her (also Song 8:2). The reference to
the "mother's house" is unusual (Ruth 1:8), particularly given the standard phrase used to designate ancient Israel's most basic family unit, the
"father's house."[11] But "father" is never mentioned in the Song, while the
mother is referenced seven times no less. Patriarchal practice in biblical
times dictated that the bride leave her own family and marry into the
groom's. But not here: it is the woman who boldly takes the initiative and
possesses the man! It is the mother who defines the household. Such love
upends patriarchal convention.[12] In the maternal bedroom, the man is,
as it were, folded back into the womb. Like mother, like daughter: the
daughter's boldness attests to her mother's virility (Song 3:4; 6:9; 8:5).
The date does not fall far from the palm tree.

11. See Meyers, "To Her Mother's House," esp. 45-47.
12. That is not to say that the woman in the Song is *free* from patriarchal constraints.
She does not have the freedom of movement that the man has, who is frequently found
leaping or bounding over mountains. The woman, on the other hand, is abused by men (the
sentinels) as she wanders the city at night in search of her beloved (5:7). For discussion and
critique, see Exum, *Song of Songs*, 25-28, 80-81.

Awakening the Senses

The Song excels in the art of arousal. Its poetry revels in imagery designed to awaken and intoxicate the senses: sight, taste, smell, touch, and hearing. The body and all its senses are engaged in deep desire and erotic arousal.

Smell and Taste

The sense of smell is featured prominently in the Song, and no wonder. Smell is a supremely powerful sense, for it can evoke a wide range of responses: from revulsion to arousal to even distant memories. Certain fragrances are designed to be highly arousing; love potions they are. "While the king was on his couch, my nard gave forth its fragrance" (1:12). With such costly perfume, of Indian origin, the "king" presumably took notice.[13] Throughout the Song, fragrance is shared by both the man and the woman. "Your anointing oils yield sweet fragrance, your name is perfume emptied out. No wonder the maidens love you," the woman declares of her beloved (1:3). She praises her lover as a "bag of myrrh lodged between my breasts" or as "a cluster of henna blossoms in the vineyards of En-gedi" (1:13-14), a lush oasis located west of the Dead Sea.

The sweet smell of love, thus, is carried not only by perfume worn upon the body. It is also borne by nature, the source of all fragrances:

> The fig tree forms its figs,
>   and the vines in blossom give forth fragrance;
> Arise, my love, my friend,
>   and come away. (2:13)

> Your breasts are like two fawns,
>   twins of a gazelle browsing among the lilies.
> When the day breathes and the shadows flee,
>   I will go to the mountain of myrrh and the hill of frankincense.
>
> (4:5-6)

---

13. The identity of the king is debated. While the royal title most likely refers to the woman's beloved as a term of extravagant admiration, there is a strand of interpretation that posits King Solomon as a third character, who tries to woo the woman from the shepherd (see Pope, *Song of Songs*, 347).

Not only are the woman's breasts likened to wild and agile animals, they are also likened to the mountains and hills that yield costly fragrances.

As one might expect, the senses of taste and smell find their convergence in a number of passages. Taste and smell are entwined in the man's praise of the woman's love:

> How beautiful is your love, my sister, bride!
>> How much sweeter is your love than wine,
>>> and the fragrance of your oils than any spice!
> Your lips drip nectar, my bride;
>> honey and milk are under your tongue;
>>> the scent of your robes is like that of Lebanon. (4:10-11)

Likewise:

> I come to my garden, my sister and bride;
>> I gather my myrrh with my spice, I eat my honeycomb with my
>> honey,
> I drink my wine with my milk.
>> Eat, friends, drink, and get drunk with love. (5:1)

Those substances that stimulate both taste and smell also involve another powerful sense: touch.[14] Love as embodied by the woman is wet, slippery, and sticky, brought together in an intoxicating mix of taste, touch, and smell. Elsewhere, the woman is described as flowing water: "A garden fountain, a well of fresh waters flowing from Lebanon" (4:15). She is pure water that sustains and refreshes, slaking the lover's thirst, satisfying his desire.

The well-tended garden is a place filled with fruit and fragrance. So also is the woman's body:

> Awake, O north wind, and come, O south wind!
>> Blow upon my garden so that its fragrance may spread abroad.
> Let my beloved come to his garden,
>> and taste its choicest fruits. (4:16)

The woman speaks of what she offers her lover: "choicest fruits." But she also revels in what he offers her, "his fruit":

14. My thanks to Christine Roy Yoder for pointing this out.

With great delight I sit in his shadow;
    his fruit is sweet to my taste.
He took me to the banqueting house,
    and his banner over me was love.
Sustain me with raisin cakes, refresh me with apples;
    for I swoon with love. (2:3b-5)

Love is cast as delectable sustenance.

May your breasts be like clusters of the vine,
    and the scent of your breath like apples,
and your mouth like choicest wine flowing smoothly for lovers,
    gliding over lips and teeth. (7:8-9)

As the man ascends from the woman's breasts to her mouth, grapes and apples turn to wine, indeed "the best wine" (cf. 1:2; 4:10). "There is nothing better," proclaims Qoheleth, than "to eat and drink" (Eccles. 2:24). All the better when such simple acts of sustenance turn so seductive!

Touch

The Song of Songs begins with kissing: "Let him kiss me with the kisses of his mouth! For your love is sweeter than wine" (Song 1:2; see also 7:9; 8:1). Kissing without restraint: "If I found you outside, I would kiss you, and no one would despise me" (8:1). And then there is the longed-for embrace: "O that his left hand were under my head, and his right hand embraced me!" (2:6; 8:3). There is no substitute for physical contact, and once the opportunity arises, the woman proclaims: "When I found the one I love, I held him and would not let him go until I brought him into my mother's house" (3:4). The embrace of love, more a tenacious seizing than a gentle hug, refuses to let go. Elsewhere, the woman evokes the maternal scene of nurture at her "mother's breasts" for her beloved (8:1).

    Anatomically, the hand is particularly sensitive to touch. It is featured, both the man's and the woman's, in that enigmatic passage about the locked door, cited above (5:4-5). In this scene, both hands are in action, with strikingly different roles: the man's hand suggests penetration; the woman's hand implies openness, wet and receptive. The double entendre is unmistakable: hand in hand points to intercourse, touch of the most intimate kind, but in this case it ends in failure. Not every sexual encounter finds fulfillment, the text acknowledges. But the longing for intimate touch, the text also claims, endures.

Sight

Sight may very well be the most prominent sense referenced in the Song. Exclamations of visual beauty frequently punctuate the poetry with enthusiastic calls to attention: "*Voila,* you [*hinnekah*] are beautiful!" (e.g., 1:16; 4:1); "Look!" (*hinneh;* e.g., 2:8-9, 3:7; cf. 11). In addition to the parts of the body described so vividly and metaphorically, the Song devotes much attention to the appearance of the body as a whole:

> I am dark and beautiful, O daughters of Jerusalem,
>> like the tents of Kedar, like the curtains of Solomon.
> Do not stare at me because I am dark,
>> because the sun has gazed on me. (1:5-6)

Darkened by the sun, the woman affirms her own beauty, likening herself to the curtains that cordon the Holy of Holies in Solomon's temple, the inner sanctum. As the man compares the woman to "a mare among Pharaoh's chariots" (1:9), so the woman compares him to a "gazelle" and "young stag," "leaping upon the mountains, bounding over the hills" (2:8b-9; 8:14). The man's description of the woman may refer to the practice of an enemy army sending a mare in heat to the other side, driving the warhorses wild.[15] Or it may simply refer to a mare adorned in finery fit for a king. The power of sight and, perhaps, that of smell.

In intimately parallel fashion the man and the woman share "equal sights" of each other, as evident also in the following passage, split by two different voices:

> As a lily among brambles,
>> so is my friend among maidens.
> As an apple tree among the trees of the forest,
>> so is my beloved among young men. (2:2-3)

The lily and the apple tree, the woman and the man: by their arresting beauty they are standouts among their peers.

---

15. So Pope, *Song of Songs,* 338-39.

Hearing

The woman yearns for the "voice of [her] beloved" (2:8). The man exclaims how "sweet" is her voice (2:14). Their voices are matched by nature's voices: "The flowers appear in the land; the time of singing has arrived, and the voice of the turtledove is heard throughout our land" (2:12). As the season of love, spring ushers in new scents, sights, *and* sounds. The longing to hear the other's voice is indispensable to the lover's desire for the other. "O you who dwell in the gardens, my companions are listening for your voice; let me hear it," pleads the man (8:13). "His speech is most sweet, and all of him is desirable," exclaims the woman (5:16a). So desirable is the voice of the other that it can be tasted.

The "sweet" voice of the other signifies attentive, undivided presence, altogether desired:

> My dove, in the clefts of the rock,
>   in the coverts of the cliff,
> show me your face,
>   let me hear your voice;
> for your voice is sweet,
>   and your face is beautiful. (2:14)

In this poignant passage, voice and face, the auditory and the visual, are poetically conjoined, necessarily so. For what is a face without voice? What, indeed, is love without voice?

In the Garden

The desired setting of the Song is itself a thing of wonder. One might call it the Song's "centerfold." It is the central place of love, as expressed in the female chorus:

> Where has your beloved gone, most beautiful among women?
>   Which way has your beloved turned, that we may seek him with you?
> My beloved has gone down to his garden, to the beds of spices,
>   to pasture (his flock) in the gardens, to gather lilies. (6:1-2)

The garden is much more than a setting; it is a metaphor for the woman:

> A garden locked is my sister and bride,
>   a garden locked, a fountain sealed.
> Your plants are an orchard of pomegranates,
>   with all choicest fruits, henna with nard,
> nard and saffron, calamus and cinnamon,
>   with all trees of frankincense, with myrrh and aloes,
>   with all the finest spices —
> a garden fountain, a well of fresh water,
>   flowing from Lebanon. (4:12-15)

When the woman beckons the man to "come to his garden and eat its choicest fruits" (2:5), it is an invitation to lovemaking. She is the garden; he is the shepherd who pastures his flock in the garden. In the garden, the woman is whisked away by her "desire":

> I went down to the nut orchard to look at the blossoms of the valley,
>   to see if the vines had budded,
>   and the pomegranates were in bloom.
> Unawares,
>   my desire [*nephesh*] set me amid the chariots with the prince.[16]
> Come back, come back, O Shulammite!
>   Come back, come back, that we may gaze upon you.
> Why should you gaze upon the Shulammite,
>   as upon a dance before two armies? (6:11-13)

The woman, a Shulammite,[17] is whisked away by her "desire." The word here for "desire" can also mean "appetite" as well as "inner being" or "life-force" *(nephesh)*. "Desire" is the best translation here (New Revised Standard Version has "fancy"). It is the force of uncontrollable passion that transports the self, pulling and pushing the subject toward the object of longing. By her desire, the woman is placed beside her "prince." Now she is gone, leaving her female peers begging her to come back.

The man boasts of his one vineyard, his "very own," over and against the thousand Solomon once had:

---

16. This verse is difficult to translate, perhaps due to textual corruption. For discussion, see Exum, *Song of Songs,* 211, 213, 222-25.

17. An unknown ethnic or geographical designation, or perhaps a play on Solomon's name.

> Solomon had a vineyard at Baal-hamon; he entrusted the vineyard
>   to keepers;
>   each one was to bring a thousand pieces of silver in exchange for
>   its fruit.
> But my vineyard, my very own, is for myself;
>   you, O Solomon, may have the thousand,
>   and the keepers of the fruit two hundred! (8:11-12)

Cultivating the metaphor of the vineyard, the man boasts of his love for one woman over and against Solomon's many wives (1 Kings 11:3). His one companion is his utmost desire, the one who "dwells in the gardens" (8:13). Such is the "lushness of sexual exclusivity."[18] Committed lovers are garden dwellers, so the Song professes, for in the garden love is ever renewed. The lovers' bed and abode construct a verdant grove: "Our couch is green; cedars are the beams of our house; cypresses are our rafters" (1:16-17). Love's intimacy turns a home into a garden grove; it marks a return to Eden, where the primal man proclaimed his joy over the primal woman, discovering the common bond between them: "flesh of my flesh" (Gen. 2:23). One flesh in two; two in one, two hearts sealed together. Cultivated love. So it was in the beginning; so it shall be forever more:

> Set me as a seal upon your heart, as a seal upon your arm;
>   for love is as fierce as death, passion as severe as Sheol.[19]
>   Its flames are flames of fire, a raging flame.
> Mighty waters cannot quench love,
>   neither can floods drown it. (8:6-7a)

And it is in the garden that death meets its match in love's "raging flame."[20] Eden's secret garden becomes love's open garden in the union of two selves, the portal to paradise.

---

18. Ellen F. Davis, *Proverbs, Ecclesiastes, and the Song of Songs,* Westminster Bible Companion (Louisville: Westminster John Knox, 2000), 235. See also 5:1; 6:9.

19. The abode of the dead.

20. Literally, the "flame of YH" *(shalhebetyah),* short for YHWH, usually translated "LORD." This is the only overt allusion to God in the Song of Songs. Some interpreters suggest a wordplay on two epithets for God in the unusual oath formula in 2:7 and 3:5: "gazelles" *(tseba'ot)* and the Lord of Hosts *(tseba'ot),* as well as "wild does" *(aylot hassadeh)* and "God Almighty" *(el shadday).* If so, these veiled references to God exhibit great playfulness.

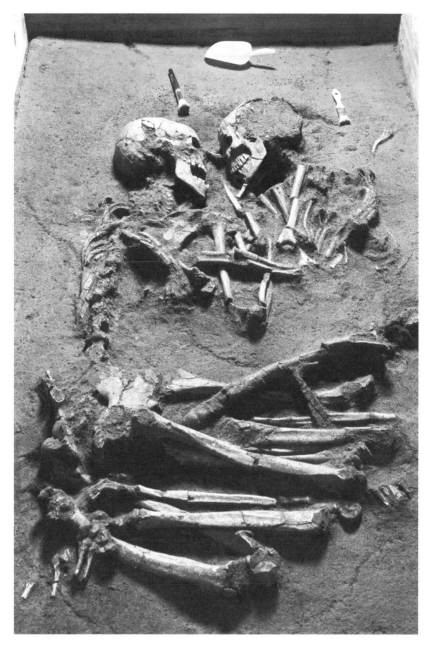

The so-called "Lovers of Valdaro" discovered in a Neolithic tomb near Mantova, Italy. *Courtesy of Pasquale Sorrentino/Science Source.*

Love beyond Sex

The Song ends on a note of deep longing: "Take flight, my love, and be like a gazelle" (8:14). Is the woman sending her beloved away, or is she beckoning him to return? The Song leaves the reader without closure, without a final fulfillment of desire, just as it began *in medias res* in a shower of kisses. The Song's lack of a beginning and an ending makes the Song a perpetual cycle of unabated desire.

There is no "and they lived happily ever after" here. The Song is no fairy tale romance. Rather, it sings an ongoing dialogue of restless desire, of desire ever waiting, ever imagining, ever reaching, ever elusive, all stark and vivid testimony to the irresistible lure of love. The millennia-long appeal of the Song is itself a testament to love's enduring power, love as "fierce as death." Such a compelling vision of mutual love lives on as long as the Song is read and heard. Indeed, the vision does more than endure; it expands and deepens with later generations of readers. As archetypal lovers, the man and the woman take on added identities. Jewish and Christian readings from early on have broadened the book's appeal to include the love between God and Israel and between Christ and the church, respectively. The power of erotic love leads to something even deeper, to the ultimacy of desire itself, to transcendent desire.

Desire, whether conscious or unconscious, determines most of what we do, whether you are a Freudian or a Skinnerian, monk or married, mystic or mathematician. Though focused on human desire for erotic companionship, the Song's poetry is so powerfully evocative that countless readers have found their desire for God (re)kindled, more an expansion and deepening of desire rather than a suppression of desire. In the broadest of terms, the Song arouses desire for the Other, for reaching beyond the confines of the self for the sake of intimacy with Another. And for those who find God as their ultimate desire, the Song provides rich support, indeed fuel for the "raging flame," the flame of God. Read in this way, the Song opens up God's *eros* for the world and the world's passionate yearning for God. The Song of Songs, in other words, anticipates the Love of loves:

> Take flight, my love, and be like a gazelle
>> or a young stag upon the mountains of spices! (Song 8:14)

> "Surely I am coming soon."
>> Amen. Come, Lord Jesus! (Rev. 22:20)

10. *Prophetic Wonder*

Voila, I am doing a new thing! Now it's springing forth!
  Do you not know it?

Isaiah 43:19a

Prophets are well known for their pronouncements of doom and gloom.
They are typically depicted in popular media as sullen characters screaming at the top of their lungs or wearing placards announcing the end of
the world. Such an impoverished view! The prophets of old were inspired
poets caught up in God's imaginative, passionate vision of justice and compassion. While many spouted harsh judgments, others joyfully announced
salvation and offered words of comfort (e.g., Amos 9:11-15; Isa. 40:1-5; Jer.
31:7-17). Their words reflected the volatile course of history and the fickle
conduct of their people. The prophets fully acknowledged that "shift happens," shifts even in God's word.

Prophets, thus, did not utter *timeless* truths so much as they delivered *timely* truths.[1] Their words were on target. But while their messages
differed, the prophets shared one thing in common: an overwhelming
sense of awe of God at work in the world, of God involved in the fray of
a community's life. Their prophetic commissions (those, at least, that are

---

1. Walter Brueggemann explores this thoroughly in his discussion of Jeremiah's message in "The Book of Jeremiah: Portrait of the Prophet," *Interpretation* 37 (1983): 130-45 at
144.

recounted in Scripture) revel in the fearful wonder of being in God's presence: the burning bush on sacred ground (Exod. 3), the enthroned God in the temple (Isa. 6), God's heavenly chariot hovering among the exiles (Ezek. 1–2). Such visions inspired fear, even terror, but they ultimately proved irresistible. In these terribly wondrous encounters, the prophets became possessed by God's pathos for a people,[2] and they channeled that pathos into the poetic cadences of their imaginative discourse.[3]

I have chosen two prophetic texts, each one wildly different from the other in both message and context. Over two centuries separated these two prophets. Their respective callings placed them over five hundred miles apart. And in their messages each packed a bomb of bewilderment.

God's "New Thing"

The first text comes from a prophet of the exile. In the aftermath of Babylonian invasion, Zion (Jerusalem) was left in ruins, and many of those who survived were deported to eke out their existence on foreign soil, the land of their oppressors. Such is where we find this anonymous prophet: among the exiles settled in or near Babylon.[4] Wracked by doubt over the ability of God to do much of anything, many survivors concluded that, in the words of another exilic prophet, "The LORD has forsaken the land; the LORD does not see" (Ezek. 9:9). The prophet in Isaiah employs a special term to describe the kind of desolation resulting from God's abandonment of the land: *tohu* or "waste" (Isa. 40:17, 23; 41:29; 45:18-19; 49:4), comparable to what is described in Genesis 1:2 *(tohu wabohu),* except without the waters. But it is in the midst of such godforsaken "waste" that this prophet utters a promise so audacious that only the wildest imagination can entertain it:

> Thus says the LORD,
> the one who makes a way in the sea,

2. See Abraham Joshua Heschel's treatment of the prophets as purveyors of God's pathos in *The Prophets* (New York: Harper, 1969), 1.3-26.

3. For a brilliant delineation of the prophets' imagination in communicating alternative visions of life, see Walter Brueggemann, *The Prophetic Imagination,* 2nd ed. (Minneapolis: Fortress, 2001).

4. This "anonymous" prophet is responsible for at least chapters 40–55 of Isaiah, which reflect a historical context much later than and far different from the historical prophet Isaiah of the eighth century.

a path through the mighty waters,
who draws out chariot and horse,
army and warrior together.
(But) they lie down, unable to rise;
they are extinguished, snuffed out like a wick.
"Do not remember the former things,
or ponder the things of old.
Voila, I am doing a new thing!
Now it's springing forth! Do you not know it?
I will make a way in the wilderness,
rivers in the desert.
The wild animals will honor me,
(including) the jackals and the ostriches;
for I provide water in the wilderness, rivers in the desert,
to give drink to my chosen people. . . ." (Isa. 43:16-20)

God announces "a new thing," something so radical, so unprecedented, that it is meant to replace the past. Of all the things that God commands to be forgotten, it is the exodus of old, the most foundational event in all of ancient Israel's history, the event of God parting the sea to make a dry "path" for fleeing refugees. In the prophet's version, it is entirely God's doing that Egypt's military might is mustered, and it is also God's doing that Egypt's might is wiped out, "snuffed out like a wick." Why on earth, then, would God want this tremendous event of triumph wiped from memory, an event whose legacy constitutes Israel's own identity as a freed people? Could it be that such memory of past deliverance has itself become enslaving, that it has become so rigid in the mind of the exiles that it prevents them from recognizing God doing a "new thing," blazing a new path of deliverance? How could that be? One can only wonder.

In any case, the old gives way while the new "springs forth." The prophet announces a new exodus, an exodus from the bondage of Babylon. Although announced as utterly unprecedented, there is actually more than meets the eye. Below the surface of the prophet's radical rhetoric lies a subtle connection between the old and the new. Therein lies the prophet's ingenuity, an ingenuity of the most disingenuous kind. Scratch the surface and you find that this utterly "new" exodus is actually a mirror image of the old! The elements of sea and land remain, but now they are reversed: whereas the mighty waters were split by a dry path to provide safe passage for a people in the old exodus, now rivers cut through the parched wasteland, providing sustenance and prompting praise from even wild animals. The new exodus is the reversal of the old, while the old actually serves as a precursor to the new. The pattern of safe and sustaining passage endures, whether old or new. Only the roles have been reversed, those of water and land. As radical as it is, the new is *not* created from nothing *(ex nihilo)*, neither does it simply appear out of the blue. Rather, the new is created from the old *(ex vetere)*. The new is both a rearrangement of the old and a radical departure from it. And therein lies the wonder. The prophet enables his fellow exiles to welcome the new without alienating the old while embracing what lies ahead for what it truly is: something robustly and profoundly new wrought by God.

The Sound of Justice

The other prophetic passage also has to do with water, and it comes from Amos, an agriculturalist by profession (1:1; 7:14). Although he sees himself as no prophet for profit, Amos does win the prize for perfecting divine judgment into an art form, complete with incisive imagery and an occasional touch of sarcasm. Indeed, this self-professed "dresser of sycamore trees" excels at dressing down his audience in surprising ways. He is quite adept at delivering rhetorical surprises, setting up his audience to expect one thing and then throwing a punch seemingly out of nowhere (e.g., 3:1-2; 5:18-20). No wonder Amaziah, the high priest at Bethel, wanted him to hightail it back to Judah, for his words constituted a threat to the kingdom and, the priest reasoned, a threat to Amos himself, now that he was fast becoming a wanted man. But the shepherd from Tekoa continued to prophesy doom for a nation at the peak of its power because of rampant injustice against the poor. Such is the basis for the following judgment. Amos dares to speak on behalf of God:

> I hate, I abhor your festivals;
> I cannot stand your solemn assemblies.
> Even though you offer me your burnt and grain offerings,
> I will not accept them;
> the well-being offerings of your fatted animals
> I refuse to look upon.
> Remove from me the noise of your songs;
> I will not listen to the melody of your harps.

But let justice cascade down like waters,
   and righteousness like a perennial torrent. (5:21-24)

Through this shepherd, God does not mince words. Worship seems to be rejected outright by God, in all its dimensions: from offerings of various kinds to singing praise with musical accompaniment. It is all found unacceptable whether by sight, smell, or sound, a total sensorial disgust on the part of the divine. Why? Is it because God hates worship as a matter of principle, or is it the *kind* of worship God sees practiced that is loathed? One wonders. I would like to think the latter, but I'm not so sure: the elements of worship listed in the judgment seem quite comprehensive, even as they are deemed reprehensible. Amos excels at making the reader squirm with wondering. The last two verses are the most telling. What is worship, the text asks, without the music and the singing, without the sacrificial offerings and festive liturgies? Take it all away, strip worship of all its trappings, every bit of it, and what do you have left? Perhaps nothing at all.

Or is there in God's eyes (and ears and nose) something essential to worship, a critical, missing element that undergirds it all? Take away the music and the singing, and what does God hope to hear? Does God prefer absolute silence? As the last verse makes all too clear, God does prefer to hear a sound, the "sound" of justice, likened to the roar of gushing, cascading waters, the rumbling roar of a torrent that never subsides, a wadi never running dry. And how is justice related to rushing water? Is it destructive or sustaining, overwhelming or satisfying? The prophet leaves us with the ambiguity of such forceful imagery to ponder. Perhaps it depends on where one stands in the water, where one is situated in relation to the rich and the poor, the issue that most deeply concerns the prophet throughout his book. In any case, the justice that Amos propounds requires change; it is not satisfied with maintaining the status quo.

Amos leaves open the issue as to whether worship and justice are themselves relatable. If they are, what then does worship look like, sound like, smell like when it is informed by, motivated by, shaped by justice? Are the songs sung differently, the sacrificial offerings presented in some other fashion? Are the prayers any different? One wonders. But one thing is clear: in God's ears what is said and sung in worship is mere noise without the accompanying roar of mighty waters. Without justice, worship stinks. With justice, worship works. Worship can no longer be business as usual. God longs for something new.

Both Amos of the eighth century and "Isaiah" of the exile are heralds of divine desire: God's longing to liberate and God's passion for justice. Both prophets invite us to wonder hard at what justice and liberation look like, indeed feel like, today. These prophets of old, it turns out, are prophets of the new, of the new imagined in and for their respective contexts. In their cases, flowing, gushing water figures prominently in the shaping of the moral imagination. In one case, water reverses an old paradigm of salvation; in the other, it reconfigures what it means to worship. Both prophets present radically new visions using a single, common image. Once unleashed, water always finds a way. So also the prophetic word.

11. *Incarnational Wonder*

JOHN 1:1-18

The Word became flesh and moved into the neighborhood.

John 1:14

In its first eighteen verses, the Gospel of John tells a Christmas story unlike any other, a *cosmic* Christmas. It begins *sans* shepherds, without an evil king, and minus even a manger. In their stead, God's radiant glory and grace occupy center stage. The star of Bethlehem is replaced with God's life-giving light. Under John's direction, the Christmas event is accompanied not by "What Child Is This?" to the delicate tune of Greensleeves but by something comparable to the mighty cadences of Richard Strauss's symphonic tone poem *Also Sprach Zarathustra*. John's prologue is essentially "A God Odyssey" announced with the blaring of trumpets and crashing symbols.

Behind John's thunderous opening, however, one can hear the strains of familiar texts. John 1 is a literary echo chamber. Genesis and Proverbs resound throughout John's prologue, a literary mashup yielding a whole new text. The first verse of Genesis, for example, is turned into a philosophical pronouncement. Instead of "in the beginning when God created," we read: "In the beginning was the Word [*logos*]." It is as if John had peeked behind the "beginning" of Genesis 1, behind the dark and watery void, before God's first act of creation, and discovered something so foundational, so deep, that it could account for all creation. Behold the *Logos!* Typically translated "Word," *logos* comes from Greek Stoic philosophy and refers to the structuring principle of the universe that makes all life possible. By invoking the *Logos,* John claims a robust rationale for all creation. Call it God's Grand Unifying Principle (aka GUP). But *Logos* in John is more than a formal abstraction, more than a grand unified theory of everything as pursued by physicists (aka GUT). No, the *Logos* is embodied.

According to Genesis 1, God created by verbal edict. With a little help from the Stoics, John takes up this theme of creation by word and turns it into a cosmic code and then into a person. John declares that "all things came into being by" the *Logos* (John 1:3), recalling Proverbs 3:19:

> The LORD founded the earth by wisdom;
> by understanding he established the heavens.

As Wisdom was instrumental in God's act of creation, so also the *Logos,* according to John. The *Logos* in John corresponds to Wisdom in Proverbs. As in the case of Wisdom, the identity of the *Logos* traffics between the "what" and the "who," between an abstraction and a personification. But John presses further: the *Logos* is no mere personified metaphor but an actual life-and-blood person, the divine made carnal (John 1:14). And the name of this person? That is not divulged until the end (1:17).

Legacy of Light and Love

To get from principle to person, John offers the central metaphor of light, the "light of all peoples," the light that darkness cannot "overcome," "the light of the world," as Jesus later says of himself (8:12; 9:5). Such cosmic light has its own sapiential hue: this is the light that "enlightens everyone" (1:9), the light that instructs and, moreover, generates life (1:5). Cosmologically, life is light's legacy. Christologically, it is *new* life that is light's legacy.

Christ is the sign, act, and very embodiment of God's love for the world (3:16), a love that stretches back to the very origin of the cosmos. "In the beginning" God built a cosmic temple (see chapter 1), but the question is left open whether or when God would actually enter creation. According to John, that time has arrived. In Christ, God formally makes an entrance into the cosmic sanctuary, summed up in 1:14:

> The Word became flesh and lived among us. (New Revised Standard Version)

Or better translations:

> The Word became flesh and made his dwelling among us. (New International Version)

> The Word became flesh and made his home among us. (Common English Bible)

The second verb in Greek literally means to "pitch one's tent" or to "tabernacle" *(skenoō)*. In other words, "the Word became flesh and moved into the neighborhood" (Last Year's Christmas Carol).[1]

Legacy of Flesh

In Christ, divinity does not hide behind or suspend itself above "flesh" *(sarx)* but instead becomes flesh. God became flesh to dignify all flesh. "Flesh" refers to the physicality of existence. Flesh is by nature frail; it decays and decomposes, reverting to "dust" or dirt (Gen. 3:19). Flesh is emblematic of finitude, not just human flesh but that of all physical existence. Flesh, biblically speaking, is shared by all life. According to Genesis 2, both the human and the nonhuman creatures share the same substance: all are made from dirt (see chapter 2). Groundlings they all are. So the Word became dirt/flesh and took up residence on earth. Incarnation ("enfleshment") means setting down roots in the soil as well as setting up shop at the street corner. Incarnation is God moving into the neighborhood. In Christ, God has made a home on earth, like Wisdom building her house of seven pillars right around the corner and flinging wide the doors (Prov. 9:1-6).

John's bold claim is that the divine and infinite *Logos* took on finite existence. The incarnation is God not just *getting* dirty by working in the garden (Gen. 2); it is God *becoming* dirt by fully entering creation. Indeed, the "flesh" of God's "Word" is not confined to Jesus' own skin; it extends to all of life, all "flesh." The mystery of the incarnation can be summed up simply as follows:

> In Christ, the creator of all has become the creature for all.

1. Thanks to Steve and Sharol Hayner. It is adapted from *The Message.*

Or even more succinctly: the creator becomes created. To be human is, as with all life, to be created: to be conceived, gestated, birthed, to grow up, and to die. God in Christ does all that, experiences all that. God in Christ experiences created life, from heartbeat to headache. God becomes created: the Word made flesh for a world made of flesh. In Christ, God becomes conjoined to all creation, and not just to one part of it. God's embodiment in Jesus Christ establishes once and for all a divine link with the body, and all bodies, of the world.

Biologists refer to DNA, the genetic thread that connects all life as we know it. DNA is life-bearing, life-determining information. It points, one could say, to creation by code, by "word." Through our DNA, humans are kin not only to the chimpanzee *(Pan troglodytes)* and the bonobo *(Pan paniscus),* our closest evolutionary cousins, but also to elephants, houseflies, and magnolias. Biology reveals how deeply interconnected all life is, deeper than the gospel evangelist could ever have imagined. To speak of the divine *Logos* becoming flesh, of the deity becoming dirt, is to claim that God has come to embrace the very stuff of life, tissue and sinew, blood and bone. God has not just come down to earth, as on a mountaintop; God has entered into the very depths of our DNA. God shares in our DNA and, through our DNA, the very fabric of life itself.

This is all to say that God is enfleshed not only in our uniqueness as *Homo sapiens* but also in our continuity with all living beings on earth, children of "dust" that we are.[2] Such is the legacy of evolution. "For God so loved the world." God's love for the world began in creation and was formalized in God's covenant with Noah, whereby God became irreversibly committed to the flourishing of *all* "flesh" (see chapter 6). The incarnation, then, is the climactic follow-up to God's first covenant, a cosmic covenant. God's commitment to, indeed love for, the world is now backed up bodily, with blood.

Deep Grace

The incarnation, thus, is no shallow appearance.[3] It is a theophany in the flesh, God's deepest descent into the wellspring of creaturely existence,

2. See Niels Henrik Gregersen, "Deep Incarnation: Why Evolutionary Continuity Matters in Christology," *Toronto Journal of Theology* 26 (2010): 173-88, esp. 175.

3. Indeed, the Docetists, a schismatic group condemned by the First Council of Nicea (325 C.E.), argued for just that.

including death. "The well is deep," remarks the Samaritan woman (John 4:11). So also creation's well, from which the creator fully draws and drinks. Is the incarnation simply an act of self-limitation, of the infinite turning finite? Is the incarnation God's incarceration on earth? John, however, has another word, a surprising word for God's full-bodied embrace of creaturely existence, and it has little to do with limitation: "fullness" or *pleroma* in Greek (1:16). It is from God's outward-extending abundance, from God's *pleroma* that God becomes enfleshed. Divine *pleroma* is like an aroma that fills a room, like the costly ointment Mary used to anoint Jesus' feet: "The house was filled [*eplerothe*] with the fragrance of the perfume" (John 12:3). Or like God's glory, which "filled the tabernacle" such that Moses himself could not enter (Exod. 40:34-25). God's "fullness" fills life *and* death. The aroma from Mary's ointment prepares for burial, says Jesus (John 12:7). Such "fullness" points toward Jesus' death, which in turn marks Christ's glorification, according to John (12:28; 21:19). Such is the paradox of deep grace. In the "fullness" of the incarnation, God's presence fills the earth, but at great cost, not to the earth but to God. The depth of God's incarnation in Christ, as deep as death, reflects the cosmic breadth of God's saving love. "For God so loved the world [*kosmos*]."

Such is the way of God's glory: "the whole earth is full of his glory," sing the winged seraphim in the temple (Isa. 6:3). But the world as we know it is not (yet) all "glory," and John acknowledges this. There is "darkness" (John 1:3); there is rejection (1:10-11). Having moved into the neighborhood, God in Christ faces an eviction notice and ultimately a death sentence. Christ's various acts of ministry in John's Gospel, from turning water into wine at Cana to cleansing the temple, from the healings to the feedings, are all life-giving works of the "light of the world." And when Jesus utters his last words on the cross in 19:30, "It is finished [*tetelestai*]," reverberations of God's completion of the cosmos can be heard all the way from Genesis.[4] For John, the cross marks the beginning of a new completion, a new Sabbath,[5] for the world that God so loves. Christ's incarnation initiates it; Christ's death completes it, and a new creation is given birth. Like a child in a manger.

---

4. The Septuagint employs the related verb *synteleō* in Gen. 2:1-2.
5. See Gen. 2:1-3. See the theme of Sabbath "rest" in Heb. 4:1-11.

12. *Christic and Cosmic Wonder*

COLOSSIANS 1:15-20

He is before all things, and in him all things hold together.

Colossians 1:17

Some of the best theology is done in hymns, not just in creeds, encyclicals, books, and the occasional sermon. Read a portion of any hymnbook, and you'll be amazed at what goes on in the words featured beneath the melody: poetry wedded to profundity. I am convinced that good theology is the kind of theology that sings, whether in joyous praise or in haunting lament, or somewhere in between. Theology cannot afford to be dull and solemn, weighed down with tedious hair splitting and convoluted syntax. Good theology aims to set the heart on fire and inspires the mouth to sing.

The following six-verse passage from the first chapter of Colossians was meant to do just that, to be sung with wonder. It is one of the earliest texts of the New Testament, a hymn embedded in a letter to the church in Colossae, a once-important trading center in Asia Minor that was severely damaged by an earthquake in 60–61 c.e. The letter's distinctive language leads some scholars to believe that one of Paul's students, rather than Paul himself, wrote it. In any case, the hymn itself was evidently not penned by the letter's author but came from, or at least was used by, the Colossian congregation. Unfortunately, we do not know the melody, but the words preserved in this most ancient of Christian hymns are priceless:

> He is the image of the invisible God,
> > the firstborn of all creation;
> for in him all things in heaven and on earth were created, things
> > > visible and invisible,
> > whether thrones or dominions or rulers or powers;
> > > all things have been created through him and for him.
> He is before all things,
> > and in him all things hold together.
> He is the head of the body, the church;
> > he is the beginning, the firstborn from the dead,
> > > so that he might become preeminent in all things.
> For in him all the fullness (of God) was pleased to dwell,
> and through him to reconcile all things to himself,
> > by making peace, whether on earth or in heaven,
> > > through the blood of his cross.

This hymn is a wonder to behold, let alone sing. As John 1 attests to the marvelous depth of Christ's incarnation, so Colossians 1 proclaims the incalculable scope of Christ's salvific reach. In fact, the Christ hymn and John's prologue share much in common. Both identify Christ as the means and medium of creation. But the key to the Colossians hymn is found in one small word that is distributed no less than eight times throughout the hymn: "all" (Greek *pas*), a tiny word with infinite significance.[1] "*All* things" were created in, through, and for Christ. "*All* things" are held together in Christ and reconciled through Christ. Christ is the "firstborn of *all* creation"; Christ "is preeminent in *all* things." All in all, there is nothing that remains unrelated to the cosmic Christ. In this ancient hymn, Christ is depicted as the "goal and glue" of all creation.[2]

"All," in short, means all. The one place where "all" does not refer to the totality of creation is found in 1:19. Here this tiny word that carries such universal scope refers to the totality of God's "fullness" *(pleroma)*, the "fullness" of divinity that came to dwell *(katoikeō)* in Christ, even as, according to John, the enfleshed Word came to dwell in the world (John 1:14). An intriguing parallel is found in Matthew 23:21, where God is said to

---

1. If the last line in Col. 1:18 is an addition, as some scholars hold, then the total count would have been seven in the hymn's original form, thereby highlighting a sense of completion as in Gen. 1:1–2:3!

2. Thanks to my colleague Stanley Saunders for this felicitous phrase.

"dwell in" the temple (cf. Exod. 40:34-35). God in Christ is God "dwelling" in Christ, ever present in Christ. In Christ, God is at home, delight*fully* at home. Joy is the reason for God's work in Christ. "To dwell" and "to reconcile" — hymnic references to the incarnation and atonement — are both matters of divine delight in the Colossians hymn (Col. 1:19-20). Jesus is God's joy to the world.

Just as Genesis 1 reverberates unmistakably throughout John 1, so Proverbs 8 accompanies this hymn as its basso continuo. As Wisdom declares herself to be prior to all creation (Prov. 8:23-27a), so Christ is said to be "before all things" (Col. 1:17a). Both Wisdom and Christ manifest God's "delight" (Prov. 8:30; Col. 1:19): Wisdom delights in both God and creation; Christ is the locus of God's joy in reconciling the world. Such reconciliation, according to the hymn, builds on the affirmation that "all things hold together [*synesteken*]" in Christ (Col. 1:17). This recalls what Wisdom says about herself in Proverbs 8:30a in an ancient Greek version of the Hebrew text, the Septuagint: "I was beside [God] binding together [*harmozousa*]."[3] Here Wisdom (*sophia* in Greek) is regarded as the binding, dynamic force behind creation. So Christ in Colossians.

So what precisely is their relationship, Christ and Wisdom, the *Logos* incarnate and *Sophia* personified? They parallel each other so well that they could be considered genetic twins, identical twins even, if not for one being feminine and the other masculine. Christ, God's only begotten Son of God; Wisdom, God's only begotten Daughter. Of course, a major difference is that Wisdom, as powerful a figure as she is in Proverbs, remains a metaphor. Christ in Colossians, it turns out, is an actual person. Christ is the *human* embodiment of God's cosmic Wisdom. To put it starkly, what sets Christ apart from Wisdom is that Christ dies. Like Wisdom, Christ is the "firstborn of all creation" (Col. 1:15), but Christ is also the "firstborn of the dead" (1:18). The former gives Christ preeminence over creation, as one could say about Wisdom in Proverbs. The latter, however, gives Christ preeminence over the future.

The hymn proceeds from everything "holding together" in Christ (1:17) to God's intent for all things to be "reconciled" through Christ (1:20). The movement from one to another is by no means seamless, however. Whereas things can be held together in tension, even in conflict, reconciliation makes for harmonious relations, for perfect peace. According to the Christ hymn, such peace comes with a grave cost, the cost of the cross.

3. Or "joining together in harmony."

Reference to Christ's death is found at the climactic position in the hymn. Far from being an afterthought, the cross is actually the culmination of a series of theological touchstones featured in this ancient hymn: creation, providence, authority, and incarnation. Why did Christ die? Is it because Jesus acted as our substitute to satisfy God's wrath? Is it because God's exacting justice required recompense from sinful humanity, which God's Son chose to take upon himself? There is neither mention of God's wrath nor reference to such stringent jurisprudence in this most ancient of hymns. Any theory of "substitutionary atonement" cannot be found here. The hymn, instead, focuses singularly on the consequence of Christ's death: the reconciliation of "all things." The express purpose of the cross, in other words, is found in peacemaking. Note the poetic parallel between 1:16 and 1:20: "*all things* have been created *through him*"; "*through him* to reconcile *all things* to himself." The scope of Christ's atoning death is nothing short of cosmic. Call it "all-in-all atonement" (cf. 1 Cor. 15:28).

By way of illustration, I lift up in wonder a remarkable mid-thirteenth-century map of the world, the largest of its kind painted on thirty goatskins and nearly twelve feet in diameter, known as the *Ebstorf Mappamundi* (see p. 122).[4] It was discovered in 1830 in the Benedictine monastery in Ebstorf, Germany.[5] In the cartographic convention of its day, the map places Jerusalem squarely in the center, with the continent of Asia stretching upward (east), Africa on the right (south), and Europe on the left and downward (north and west). The map offers a comprehensive picture of the Christian world as it was known in medieval times. Included are scenes from biblical history, including Christ rising from the tomb at the center. But what is particularly striking is what is found at the map's extremities: Christ's head is on top (right next to the garden of Eden), his hands outstretched toward north and south, and his feet extending westward or downward. The entire world, both geographically and historically, is superimposed upon Christ's crucified body!

Could this map from the Middle Ages be a visual depiction of Christ "holding all things together," of Christ "reconciling all things to himself," as

4. Thanks to Stanley Saunders for directing my attention to this remarkable example of medieval Christian cartography. For discussion and visual detail, see http://blog.visualmotive.com/wp-content/uploads/2009/09/ebstorfer-mappamundi.jpg (accessed 10/21/2013).

5. Tragically, the map was destroyed in 1943 in the bombing of Hanover. For detailed discussion see http://cartographic-images.net/Cartographic_Images/224_Ebstorf_Mappa mundi.html (accessed 10/21/2013).

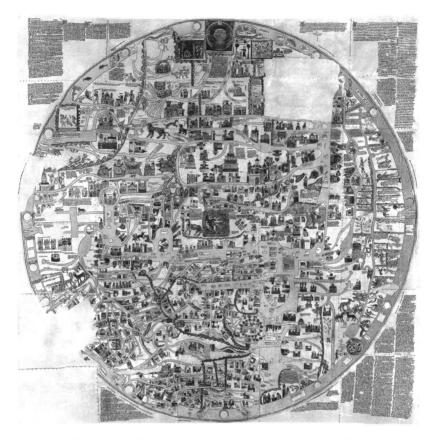

The *Ebstorf Mappamundi,* a thirteenth-century map of the world discovered in a convent in Ebstorf, Germany. Approximately 12 feet (3.6 meters) in diameter.
Credit: University of Lüneberg.

described in Colossians? Is this a medieval roadmap of the ancient Christ hymn? I wonder. Regardless, this map locates the entire world *in* Christ, *within* Christ's cosmic embrace, *upon* his body. How could that be illustrated today in light of all that we know now about the world, indeed the universe? If "all" means all, then Christ is embracing earth and all stars, Christ is holding galaxies, nebulae, and extraterrestrial life all within his outstretched arms. And closer to home, what *on earth* is included? Life in all its manifold forms. Clearly, the map needs to be redrawn, its boundaries extended and its details multiplied. Clearly, the ethical implications need to be drawn as well.

If Christ is the head of the church and the world, no less, and, according to Paul, the church is the body of Christ (1 Cor. 12:27), then the church has everything to do with the world. In this most ancient of hymns, the church is called, no less, to be the sign of the new creation in Christ, the model of "all things" reconciled and renewed. That, then, would be the church's most wondrous, most glorious calling: the beloved community with and for the biotic community, as Christ is with and for "all things." Imagine that!

13. *Terrifying Wonder*

MARK 16:1-8

So they went out and fled from the tomb,
  for terror and amazement had seized them.

Mark 16:8a

Most scholars agree that the Gospel of Mark is the Bible's earliest story of the life of Jesus. It is certainly the shortest. In comparison to the other, much lengthier Gospels, Mark offers a remarkably brief account, particularly from both ends. It lacks a Christmas story at the beginning and an Easter appearance at the end. In between, the narrative is always in a hurry to recount what Jesus is doing and saying. Indeed, among Mark's favorites words is *euthys* ("immediately"), used forty-one times throughout his short narrative. Shed of refined literary coverings and embellishments, Mark could be called the "bare-naked" Gospel streaking across the narrative stage.[1] But a word of warning: Mark's simple and stark words reflect a subtlety overlooked by many a speed reader. Although Mark's narrative style is swift and simple, one cannot read his account swiftly and simply. As in poetry, each word in Mark requires pondering.

So also each silence, including the one that concludes Mark's Gospel. The three women breathlessly approach the tomb at the break of dawn to anoint Jesus' body. Much to their surprise, they find the stone rolled

---

1. Many wonder whether the mysterious "young man" who runs away naked when Jesus is arrested is an anonymous reference to Mark himself (14:51-52).

away. Of greater surprise is finding a "young man dressed in a white robe" announcing that Jesus "has been raised" and is "going ahead . . . to Galilee," where they can go to see him (16:6-7). The women flee the tomb, "for terror [*tromos*] and amazement [*ekstasis*] had seized them; and they said nothing to anyone, for they were afraid [*phobeomai*]" (16:8). The end. Mark's Gospel concludes with stupefied silence. No resurrection appearances, not even a testimony from the women to their male counterparts. What the women witnessed at the tomb was so frightening that it rendered them mute, even though the "young man" in white charged them to tell the disciples, including Peter, where Jesus was going (16:6). But exhibiting the signs of trauma,[2] they don't tell anyone, indeed they cannot, at least by the time the curtain falls.

The Final Gap

While narrative gaps abound in ancient literature, Mark is a striking example of a work that saves its greatest gap (more like a yawning chasm) at the very end. Attempts have been made in the course of scribal transmission to fill it. There is the "shorter ending," about two verses in length, which has the women dutifully informing Peter and his cohorts, followed by Jesus sending them out to proclaim the "sacred and imperishable proclamation of salvation." There is the longer ending (twelve verses) in which Jesus appears first to Mary Magdalene, who tells others of seeing Jesus but is met with unbelief. This is followed by an appearance of Jesus to two of the disciples, who report back and are also met with unbelief. Jesus finally makes his public appearance to the disciples, chastising them for their reluctance to believe, and then commissions them to proclaim the gospel "to the whole creation." Jesus' ascension and the disciples' fulfillment of the commission concludes this extended ending.

Or look at Matthew's ending: there the women departed from the tomb "with fear and great joy [*chara*] and ran to tell his disciples" (Matt. 28:8). So much for silence-inducing terror. So what does it mean for Mark to end his account of the "good news" in fearful flight and stupefied silence? How does terror find a place at the tomb? To explore this, it helps

---

2. See the perceptive discussion on the women's trauma at the tomb in Serene Jones, *Trauma and Grace: Theology in a Ruptured World* (Louisville: Westminster John Knox, 2009), 85-89.

to look at Mark's Gospel as a whole, starting at the beginning. This earliest Gospel opens with a gathering in the wilderness (1:4-5), and it ends with flight from an empty tomb — a strange correlation. As a "no-man's-land," the wilderness in biblical tradition is often associated with emptiness and chaos, even terror, a place to avoid altogether (e.g., Job 38:25-27). Nevertheless, the opening scene in Mark's Gospel takes place in the wilderness, where a crowd is gathered to hear John the baptizer, himself a bit of a wild man, proclaiming a message of repentance and announcing Jesus' coming (1:2-8). At the other end, the Gospel concludes with a proclamation not of Jesus' coming but of his "going ahead" (16:7), an announcement met with flight and silence (16:8). Both the desert and the tomb are ominous, desolate places, but in Mark's Gospel the former is filled with people gathered to hear words in the wilderness, recalling the new exodus announced in Isaiah 40:3, and the latter features an announcement that prompts fearful flight, as if a monster had been unleashed. Gathering and dispersal: these are the bookends of Mark. It is also, not fortuitously, the framework of worship.

The Gospel of Fear

So what lies in between? The persistent theme of astonishment runs throughout Mark's account of Jesus' ministry. People are "astounded" or "spellbound" at Jesus' teaching (1:22; 6:12; 11:18; 12:17). They are "amazed" at his miracles, including exorcisms (1:27; 5:19) and healings (2:12; 5:42). Pilate is "amazed" at Jesus' silence (15:5). Amazement turns to fear as the disciples witness Jesus stilling the storm (4:40-41), walking on water (6:50), and being transfigured (9:6). Particularly telling is the setting of Jesus' third prediction of his death and resurrection:

> They were on the road, going up to Jerusalem, and Jesus was walking ahead of them [*proagō*]; they were amazed [*thambeomai*], and those who followed were afraid [*phobeomai*]. (10:32)

Jerusalem is the destination of death for Jesus, about which he again informs his disciples in the subsequent verse (also 8:31; 9:30-31). The reaction of fear is reserved for those who follow Jesus, for those who are most closely aligned with him.

Jesus stilling the storm is also telling. As the boat was flooding due to a sudden squall on the Sea of Galilee, Jesus remains asleep in the stern. The disciples awaken him: "Teacher, do you not care that we are perishing?" (4:38). Jesus rebukes the wind and the sea, and "a great calm" follows (4:39). *Now* the disciples are fearful:

> He said to them, "Why are you cowards? Have you still no faith?" And they were greatly fearful and said to one another, "Who then is this, that even the wind and the sea obey him?" (4:40-41)

Such terror *(phobos)* is reserved for after the fact, after Jesus calms the storm and upbraids them for their lack of faith, calling them "cowards" *(deiloi)*. The disciples are fear-struck, and the true object of their fear is not the storm but Jesus!

Mark's Gospel is the Gospel of fear. The other Gospels temper such fear by mixing it with joy, perplexity, and amazement (e.g., Matt. 28:8; Luke 8:25). Jesus in John's Gospel prays that his disciples not be afraid (John 14:27). But not in Mark. On the wide spectrum of wonder, the earliest evangelist prefers the extreme, fearful end when it comes to encountering Jesus. As both "Son of Man" and "Son of God," Jesus is a walking, talking theophany, whether on water or on land. Fear was elicited by God's descent on Mount Sinai (Exod. 19). The same fear is experienced at Jesus' transfiguration on a high mountain (Mark 9:2, 6). Jesus in Mark is the divine *mysterium tremendum* made human.

Fear Resisting Closure

And so what about the women's fear at the tomb? What are they afraid of? Is their fear unfounded or legitimate? Mark leaves us to wonder. What is fearful about an announcement of Jesus' resurrection? Has Jesus returned to retaliate against all who caused him to suffer unto death? Has Jesus come back as the divine warrior to take revenge on those who abandoned and denied him, including his disciples? Is there something specifically about Jesus "going ahead" *(proagō)* that provokes fear (16:7; cf. 14:28; 10:32)? Is he setting a trap in Galilee? Now all that would be cause for great fear: Jesus is back, and he's not happy! Perhaps that is something of what the women actually felt, but Mark knows better. Mark's intent is far larger; he is not simply playing upon the unfounded fears of the first witnesses. His fear has all to do with disorientation, the kind of disorientation when all sense of closure is destroyed. Mark's fearful ending is a "nonending."[3] With the finality of fear, Mark subverts the finality of an ending, leaving what happens next entirely up for grabs. Fear maintains the gap, leaving the future wide open, full of questions and possibilities. Like the female witnesses, the reader is catapulted from the tomb to imagine what might or could happen next. With this final gap left unfilled, the reader is jolted into a stupefied state of wondering. And the root of such fear is Christ's unexpected resurrection,[4] an event deemed unfathomable and insurgent, resisting all sense of closure and containment. Christ's resurrection marks the beginning of an invasion, the invasion of life in a world more comfortable with, indeed obsessed with, death.[5] Resurrection is beyond mental grasping because it heralds the unimaginable: an empty tomb emptied of death.

Ironic Fear

Fear in Mark is ironic and surprising. Indeed, Mark's Gospel is filled with irony and surprise. Demons acknowledge Jesus' true identity more readily than the disciples do (e.g., 1:22; 3:11). Jesus is hailed "King of the Jews" in utter humiliation and torture (15:2, 9, 12). A Roman centurion declares, "Truly this man was God's Son!" at the moment not of Jesus' victory but of his death on the cross (15:39). Jesus sternly warns people *not* to say anything about the miracles they have just witnessed (1:44; 7:36; 9:9). Mark's Gospel is thus a Gospel of secrecy or *mysterion* (4:11). But now, at the end, the first witnesses to the resurrection — the greatest miracle of all — are charged to proclaim something, and they don't! Through irony, Mark excels at generating literary instability and disorientation. Nothing is predictable in Mark's Gospel. His "good news" is gut wrenching.

As for Jesus' destiny with death in Jerusalem, irony reigns there too. Mark doesn't wince at bringing two ideas into direct collision: kingship and humiliation.[6] That collision occurs at the cross, where death and divinity, suffering and sonship, find their scandalous convergence. But it is

---

3. Jones, *Trauma and Grace*, 89.

4. Even if it was foretold (Mark 14:28)!

5. For a hair-raising treatment of the resurrection in Mark's Gospel, see Brian K. Blount, *Invasion of the Dead: Preaching Resurrection* (Louisville: Westminster John Knox, 2014), 80-108, in which he likens Christ's resurrection to a zombie apocalypse.

6. Donald Juel, "Christian Hope and the Denial of Death: Encountering New Testament Eschatology," in *The End of the World and the Ends of God: Science and Theology on*

not unprecedented. Mark sprinkles references to two psalms in order to provide precedence for what happens in the crucifixion. The most obvious is Jesus' cry from the cross, "My God, my God, why have you forsaken me," which directly recalls the first verse of Psalm 22.[7] In addition, the reference to the soldiers dividing up Jesus' clothes at the foot of the cross in Mark 15:24 recalls Psalm 22:18 ("they divide my clothes among themselves, and for my clothing they cast lots"), and the derision Jesus suffers while crucified in Mark 15:29-32 echoes Psalm 22:7-8:

> All who see me mock me;
>> they open (their) lips and shake their heads.
> "He has committed himself to the LORD,
>> so let him deliver him.
>> Let him save him, for he delights in him."

Finally, the attempt to give Jesus "sour wine" recalls Psalm 69:21b ("for my thirst they gave me vinegar to drink"). Both Psalm 22 and Psalm 69, both attributed to David, are anguished laments in which the cry of the afflicted is directed to God. Psalm 22 is the most agonizing, opening with the wrenching cry of divine abandonment. How can the Son of God cry this? (It is not found in Luke or John.) By reciting the cry of the psalmist, the cry of the afflicted, Christ has entered most fully into the trauma of human life, not just death in general but death by execution, in abject despair and bitter protest. Humanity's most anguished cry is now the cry of Christ, Son of God. Executed as a criminal of the state, Jesus shares in our death at its most extreme and inhumane. Call it solidarity atonement *in extremis*.[8]

What Mark also leaves unsaid may be just as important, namely how Psalm 22 concludes with unbridled thanksgiving and praise from someone delivered by God and who now beseeches the world, no less, including the dead and those unborn, to render praise to God (22:21-31). For those who have ears to hear, the psalmic echoes in Mark's passion narrative recall a

---

Eschatology, ed. John Polkinghorne and Michael Welker (Harrisburg, PA: Trinity, 2000), 171-83 at 176.

7. The crowd ironically misunderstands Jesus' cry of dereliction, thinking that he is calling upon Elijah rather than "my God" *(Eloi)* (15:35).

8. In point of fact, the formal language of atonement, as typically conceived at least, is entirely absent in Mark's account of Jesus' passion and crucifixion (Juel, "Christian Hope," 176).

seamless yet surprising move from affliction to salvation, from anguished despair to joyous thanksgiving. Psalm 22 turns on a hairpin in verse 21, a whiplash moment that immediately(!) transforms a bitter complaint and desperate petition into powerful testimony and extravagant praise:

> Save me from the mouth of the lion!
>   From the horns of the wild oxen you have answered me!

Just like that (fingers snapped).

The Big Bafflement

Mark presses Psalm 22 into service on the cross but leaves unstated how the psalm also points to Christ's resurrection, just as Mark leaves unstated what happens after the women flee stupefied from the tomb. The deafening silence of the unstated seems to be part of Mark's ploy. All signs and promises point to a glorious resurrection, whether from the psalm or from Jesus' own predictions, but Mark refuses to recount their fulfillment, refuses to wrap the story up in glory. "He is not here," and that's that. Ironically, it is an understatement of absence, rather than a glorious, awe-filled appearance, that elicits fear. For Mark, a resurrection from the dead is an incalculable event that resists all manner of closure. It is, to borrow from the language of physics, a "singularity," a moment when all the known physical laws break down, as in the Big Bang. Mark's singularity at the tomb is the Big Bafflement. While Mark's ending seems unsatisfactory by comparison to the endings found in Matthew, Luke, and John, Mark points unapologetically to the sheer unknown. Mark is content to leave it all to the trembling reader's imagination at the empty tomb, where everything we thought we knew about life has now been shattered once and for all. If there ever was a deafening silence, this is it.

So if Jesus is "not here" in the tomb, where is he? If Jesus has gone ahead to Galilee, as the young man claimed and as Jesus himself foretold prior to his death (14:28), what does that say about Mark's "end"? Here, the ending may very well circle back to the beginning: Jesus began his ministry in Galilee, proclaiming the coming of God's kingdom (1:14-15). Jesus "going ahead" to Galilee, thus, marks something of a return. Does it also take the reader back to the beginning of the Gospel, where Jesus began his ministry? Perhaps the open-ended conclusion is Mark's invitation to reread the Gospel from the beginning, but now in light of Jesus' crucifixion and resurrection. Mark's Gospel is the never-ending Gospel. Out of the tomb Jesus goes ahead to Galilee; "there you will see him." Perhaps that is the final message Mark presses upon the reader: Go ahead and see for yourself, but approach in silence. Mark may be telling us that if we don't encounter the resurrection with fearful, speechless wonder, we are as good as dead.

14. *Resurrection Wonder*

JOHN 20:1-18

> Supposing him to be the gardener, she said to him,
> "Sir, if you have carried him away, tell me where you have
>   laid him."
>
> *John 20:15*

The wonder of the word is powerfully evident in John's Gospel. "In the beginning was the Word" begins the gospel, and throughout the Gospel Jesus is full of words. Jesus' farewell discourse and prayer (14:1–17:26), for example, is without parallel in Matthew, Mark, and Luke and spans nearly four chapters, proving beyond a shadow of a doubt that "wordy" is the Lamb, wonderfully wordy. When Thomas comes to believe in the resurrected Jesus once he has seen and touched Jesus' wounds, Jesus responds with the searching question: "Have you believed because you have seen me? Blessed are those who have not seen and yet have come to believe" (20:29).

We readers of John, of course, have not seen the resurrection. None of us can lay claim to having been present at the empty tomb. But because we *hear* the ancient story passed down to us, we are more blessed than the eyewitnesses, Jesus says. Blessed are those who have heard! The playful irony is that John's account of the resurrection is full of seeing, a visual feast of details and perspectives lacking in the other Gospels. In John, the word — spoken and read — does all the seeing. Mary, the first eyewitness to the resurrection, is told to go and tell his disciples what she has *seen*

(20:17). The resurrection story, in fact, begins with each character seeing something different. So also every reader of the story.

In the Eyes of the Beholders

Here is what I see: John makes vividly clear that the story of Easter begins in a garden, which is more than just a backdrop. The story also begins in the dark, and yet Mary is able to see something, specifically something not there where it should be. The first cry that pierced that predawn Easter morning at the garden tomb was not "Christ is risen!" but "Jesus is stolen!" Mary had every reason to believe that what she saw bore the signs of a bona fide bodysnatching. And what did she see? Exhibit A: a missing stone, a gaping entrance. And for what purpose except to steal Jesus' body! She runs to tell Simon Peter and the "other disciple," and they both run to the tomb, jostling to see who gets there first. And what did they see? The first to arrive, the "other disciple," sees linen wrappings lying in the tomb. Exhibit B. And when the winded Simon Peter gets there, he sees another detail: the head cloth neatly rolled up, separated from the wrappings. Exhibit C. So far everyone has seen something different, an added detail here, another there, completing the picture of a possible crime scene . . . or the miracle of miracles.

But Mary sees something more. Once the disciples leave, it is her turn to peer into the tomb, and she sees two angels in white. Exhibit X. Another detail overlooked by the two disciples, but a detail of far greater significance. "Why are you weeping?" they ask. She clings to her own reconstruction of events: a crime has been committed, and she wants to get to the bottom of it, to retrieve the body to ensure that Jesus, her executed teacher, is given a decent burial. But before they respond, as they do in the other Gospels, Jesus himself suddenly appears. But what she sees is the gardener.

A case of mistaken identity? More likely a case of double entendre. John, through the eyes of Mary, transports us back to the primordial past, to the first garden, planted and cultivated by God. God the gardener, king of the cosmos and compost, not only plants this lush garden but also transplants this groundling, Adam, with the express purpose to "serve it and preserve it" (Gen. 2:15). God the gardener, Adam the gatherer.

God the Gardener

God, we see throughout the Bible, is no stranger to gardening, for God plants more than a pristine garden in Eden. God plants a people, and the event of the exodus is, botanically speaking, a transplantation:

> You brought them in and planted them
>> on the mountain of your inheritance,
> the place, O LORD, you made to dwell in,
>> the sanctuary, O LORD, your hands established. (Exod. 15:17)

Or as we find in a psalm:

> You pulled up a vine out of Egypt;
>> you drove out the nations and planted it.
> You cleared a place for it;
>> it took deep root and filled the land.
> The mountains were covered with its shade,
>> the mighty cedars with its branches.
> It sent out its branches to the sea,
>> and its shoots to the River. (Ps. 80:8-11)

Or from John:

> I am the true vine, and my Father is the gardener. (John 15:1)

And even from the lips of Paul, who credits God alone with growth:

> So neither the one who plants nor the one who waters is anything,
>> but only God, who makes things grow. (1 Cor. 3:7)

Gardening is a quintessentially divine activity that no other metaphor or title can fully capture. Yes, God is savior, deliverer, liberator, redeemer: God is all these, but such titles lack the sense of organic connection with the earth and with a people that only the title "gardener" can fill. To save is to save *from,* to deliver *from,* to liberate *from,* to redeem *from.* But in order to save, redeem, liberate, and deliver, God also works *with.* God works with the soil, with the fecundity of the ground, with body and flesh, to bring forth new life. God: creator, redeemer, sustainer . . . and gardener!

Organic Resurrection

It is no coincidence, then, that Mary Magdalene (mis)took Jesus as the gardener in John's account of the resurrection. An understandable mistake or no mistake at all. Things are never quite what they seem in John's Gospel. Although Mary does not immediately recognize the gardener as Jesus, she is clearly on her way toward acknowledging him as divine. Full recognition, however, comes only when her name is spoken (20:16), like the voice that called to Moses from the burning bush (Exod. 3:4). Once again, the power of the word, of Christ's word, at work! Nevertheless, Mary's initial impression of Jesus is not a false one: it contains a seed of venerable truth about God's creative power to bring forth new life. Gardeners are, after all, cultivators of life; they work with the old to raise up the new, and only God can raise a body from the soil that is our flesh. Gardeners are, in fact, practitioners of resurrection, of bringing forth new life from below, from out of the rich, decaying, organic soil. The human from the humus.

By recognizing Jesus as the gardener, Mary takes us back also to the creation of Adam, fashioned out of the "dust of the ground" as a piece of pottery and animated by God's breath. It is a striking image, so striking that even Michelangelo dared not to depict it on the ceiling of the Sistine Chapel: of God performing CPR, or more accurately CPS (cardiopulmonary "suscitation"), an intimately tactile picture of God breathing into Adam's lungs and bringing him to life (see chapter 2). Such is the way of this down-to-earth deity.

And what God does for Jesus in resurrecting him, I suspect, is no less tactile and intimate. By recalling the first garden in his resurrection account, John invites us to wonder, to imagine new life, resurrection no less, in this second garden. Perhaps it happened this way: God walks in the garden in the dead of night and removes the stone and enters the burial cave. God embraces Jesus' body, holding him tight, pressing flesh upon spirit and spirit upon flesh with the same dirty hands that fashioned Adam's "soul" from the soil. God bathes Jesus with life-giving breath that not only reanimates him but transforms him body and soul: body devoid of decay and free of limitation yet still bearing the marks of crucifixion. A resurrection, a new creation!

Make no mistake: Mary's mistake is no mistake, for John has her testifying to the saving, creative, animating, resurrecting presence of God even before she recognizes Jesus as the resurrected one. "How are the dead raised?" Paul asks. The apostle points to the seed, which must die before it bursts forth with new life (1 Cor. 15:35-36). Resurrection is organic, and the results are beyond measure. Without the seed, there would be no cedar, no majestic redwood, no mustard bush. Without the body, there would be no resurrection, no new creation. New creation bursting forth from the shell of a seed, out of the ground of dust and decay.

Resurrection, thus, is not "creation out of nothing." Resurrection is new creation out of the old. As Jesus' own body bears witness, the body that still bears the marks of the cross, resurrection is new life created from our fleshy, bony, bloody, dusty, dirty selves. No wonder, then, that Paul describes Christ's resurrection as "the firstfruits" (1 Cor. 15:20, 23). There is something boldly bodily about the resurrection. "I believe in the resurrection of the body," so declares the ancient creed. Both in this life and the next, we have our bodies — everything that makes us who we are, including our wounds.[1]

Ecology of Resurrection

But there's more. Resurrection is not limited to ourselves, and the key is found in what happens to our bodies in death. "To dust you shall return," God tells Adam (Gen. 3:19). In death, that "dust" or dirt — the basic constituent of our bodies, indeed of life itself — will become dispersed, ultimately providing the constituents for other living bodies. Such is the cycle of life and death. As the molecules of our decaying bodies become shared with future generations of life, and as our own living bodies reflect the broad evolutionary legacy of life in all its interdependence, then resurrection ultimately cannot be limited to the raising up of individual bodies. Resurrection includes the whole of life in its vast eschatological and ecological sweep, all from the simple fact that we remain, now and forevermore, tied to God's creation. Resurrection has all to do with God the creator, God the gardener. Resurrection is hands down the most miraculous act of cultivation, and it is also the most essential act of cultivation: the eruption of new life out of the soil that is our flesh. Resurrection is God's cosmic victory garden.

E. B. White speaks of his wife, Katharine, an avid gardener, who every fall without fail began to plot and to plant:

1. It is precisely Christ's wounds that make him identifiable in the eyes of Thomas. Nevertheless, wounds in the resurrection no longer have the power to define and control.

I . . . used to marvel at how unhesitatingly she would kneel in the dirt and begin grubbing about, garbed in a spotless cotton dress or a handsome tweed skirt and jacket. She simply refused to dress down to garden: she moved in elegantly and walked among her flowers as she walked among her friends — nicely dressed, perfectly poised.

The only moment in the year when she actually got herself up for gardening was on the day in fall that she had selected, in advance, for the laying out of the spring bulb garden — a crucial operation, carefully charted and full of witchcraft. . . .

Armed with a diagram and a clipboard, Katharine would get into a shabby old Brooks raincoat much too long for her, put on a little round wool hat, pull on a pair of overshoes, and proceed to the director's chair — a folding canvas thing — that had been placed for her at the edge of the plot. There she would sit, hour after hour, in the wind and the weather, while Henry Allen produced dozens of brown paper packages of new bulbs and a basketful of old ones, ready for the intricate interment. As the years went by and age overtook her, there was something comical yet touching in her bedraggled appearance on this awesome occasion . . . her studied absorption in the implausible notion that there would be yet another spring, . . . sitting there with her detailed chart under those dark skies in the dying October, calmly plotting the resurrection.[2]

So it is with God the gardener, who refuses to "dress down" and yet is no stranger to dirt. God in Christ is no stranger to flesh, the soil of our souls.

So what do *you* see in the empty tomb on that dark and misty morning?

An open entrance,
strewn linens,
two angels,
a gardener,
a teacher,
Lord and Savior,
the firstfruits,

2. E. B. White, "Introduction" to K. S. White's *Onward and Upward in the Garden*, ed. E. B. White (New York: Farrar, Straus & Giroux/Toronto: McGraw-Hill Ryerson, 1979), xvii-xix.

the tree of life,
the new creation,
or hope for the world?

I see all of the above.

15. *Communion Wonder*

LUKE 24:13-32

> Then their eyes were opened, and they recognized him,
>   and he vanished from their sight.
>
> *Luke 24:31*

Luke adds a uniquely peripatetic episode to his account of Christ's resurrection: two disciples joined by a stranger who turns out to be no stranger at all yet disappears at the very moment of recognition. Luke presents to us the mysterious case of the vanishing Christ.

While there's clearly more than meets the eye in this story, the text's mystery has equally to do with the ear. It is on an ordinary seven-mile trek that the entire journey of the biblical story is allegedly covered, and all beyond the reader's own hearing. While knowing full well that it is Jesus who walks in the guise of a stranger, the reader does not hear most of what Jesus says to the two disciples, who have no clue. So much for the omniscient reader. I would in a heartbeat give up my "superior" position as a reader and join these befuddled disciples just to listen to this stranger and hear how he interpreted the Hebrew Scriptures to make sense of Jesus' death and resurrection. Call me a bewildered biblical scholar, but I truly wonder what on earth Jesus said to these two on the road to Emmaus. What was his hermeneutical approach, his preferred reading strategy, his narrative arc? Did he begin "in the beginning" or start somewhere else? What was it exactly that made the disciples' hearts "burn" within them "while he was opening the Scriptures" to them (24:32)?

Hermeneutical Hankerings

Let's back up. Jesus overhears these two disciples talking about their leader's crucifixion and their dashed hopes. He comes as a stranger. Given the disciples' reaction, this newcomer could have been from another planet altogether: "Are you the *only* stranger . . . who does not know the things that have taken place" (24:18)? Feigning ignorance, the stranger queries ("what things?"), and the disciples recount the story of a "prophet mighty in deed and word" who was condemned to death by the religious authorities, crucified, dead, and buried. Also buried were their hopes that Jesus would "redeem Israel," that is, liberate the Jews from Roman imperial rule (24:21). Now on the third day "some women" who visited the tomb found not the body but "angels" claiming that he was alive (24:23). This, of course, required confirmation, and so it was, but only partially: no dead body but no live body. No angels either. Only an empty tomb.

Their story prompts a total stranger to upbraid them for not figuring it out, but it has nothing to do with them having missed something in the tomb or with suspicion cast upon the women's testimony. Instead, it all has to do with biblical interpretation:

> "Was it not necessary for the Christ to suffer these things and then enter into his glory?" Then beginning with Moses and all the prophets, he interpreted to them the things concerning himself in all the Scriptures. (24:26-27)

"Moses" here refers to the Torah (from Genesis to Deuteronomy), and "all the prophets" range from Isaiah to Malachi. But the stranger's exegesis doesn't stop there; it covers "all the Scriptures," which could also include Psalms and Job, for example (Luke 24:44). Although the reader does not know it until later, something was stirring within the disciples as they listened to this stranger talking up the Hebrew Scriptures: "Were not our hearts burning within us while he was talking to us on the road, while he was opening the Scriptures to us?" (24:32). The disciples were not referring to heartburn (indigestion). Their hearts were stirred by the stranger's words. "Burning" *(kaiō)* recalls the first instance of the word's use in Scripture: Moses "looked, and the bush was blazing with fire, yet it was not consumed" (Exod. 3:7). Burning bush and burning hearts: both are the start of something new. The former inaugurated Moses' mission to liberate his people. The latter imparts a new understanding of this stranger.

God's burning compassion overcomes Moses' resistant heart, preparing him to return to Egypt and bring his people out of the tomb of bondage. The Scriptures openly interpreted prepare the disciples' hearts to know who it is that has joined them from death's dark tomb.

What, then, did Jesus, the stranger, say? What specific biblical texts did he reference? Did Jesus speak of his preexistence in relation to creation in Genesis? Did he speak of his own sojourn in Egypt as a child in connection with Israel's old exodus? Did he draw from the servant poems of Isaiah to talk about his suffering and his vindication? Did he speak of himself as the "beloved" in the Song of Songs? Did he liken himself to Child Wisdom? Did he recall the lament psalms? The reader will never know, but the two disciples did, even as they did not know who was teaching them. Luke refuses to tell us what Jesus said on that seven-mile journey. Could Luke be leaving the matter of interpreting "*all* the Scriptures" wide open, open for the reader, indeed open for generations of readers to make their own connections? Luke's refusal to elucidate is an invitation to wonder. Whatever the stranger said on the road would have tied together the seemingly disparate themes of suffering and glory (24:26), a glory that does not insulate itself from suffering but rises from it, somehow, someway. And their hearts were left burning. Wonder had seized them about a stranger who allegedly knew nothing of what was going on yet seemingly knew everything about the Scriptures to interpret what was going on. Interpreting the Scriptures to interpret the world: such was and is the goal of biblical interpretation.

Communion Wonder

But it wasn't enough. The disciples' eyes are not opened until the "breaking of the bread." The four discrete acts of the host are described: taking bread, blessing it, breaking it, and giving it (24:30), a partial replication of Luke's version of the Eucharist:

> Then he took bread and, after giving thanks,
>> broke it and gave it to them, saying,
> "This is my body, which is given for you.
>> Do this in remembrance of me." (22:19; cf. 1 Cor. 11:23-26)

Did Jesus say these words in the company of these two disciples? Did he have to say them, or was the simple act of sharing sufficient to prompt the disciples' recognition? The text does not say. According to their testimony, Jesus was simply "made known to them in the breaking of the bread" (Luke 24:35). The mere act of sharing bread was enough to trigger their recognition, perhaps recalling another text about eating:

> There is nothing better for someone than to eat and drink. . . .
> This also, I saw, is from the hand of God. (Eccles. 2:24)

With a stranger hosting a simple meal, the disciples saw God's hands at work.

Eye Openings

The disciples' "eyes were opened," and at the moment of their recognition, Jesus, revealed at the table, vanishes from their sight. A wondrous paradox unfolds: knowledge and mystery, insight and no sight, converge! Indeed, paradoxes abound when eyes are opened elsewhere in Scripture. Take the first instance: "Then the eyes of both were opened, and they knew that they were naked" (Gen. 3:7). Adam and Eve tasted the fruit of "the tree of the knowledge of good and bad," and they gained enough sight to now recognize what they lacked: clothing. Their gain was also their loss. Once the disciples gain recognition of Jesus at the table, they lose him.

Another case of opened eyes occurs with the prophet Elisha and his servant at the moment of national crisis. The king of Aram and his army have surrounded the city of Dothan, where Elisha and his servant are holed up. The servant panics after seeing the city surrounded by "an army with horses and chariots." But the prophet remains calm: "Do not fear, for there are more with us than there are with them" (2 Kings 6:16):

> Then Elisha prayed: "LORD, open his eyes that he may see." So the LORD opened the servant's eyes, and he saw that the mountain was full of horses and chariots of fire surrounding Elisha. When the Arameans came down against him, Elisha prayed to the LORD, and said, "Strike this people with blindness." So he struck them with blindness as Elisha had asked. Elisha said to them, "This is not the way, and this is not the city. Follow me, and I will bring you to the man whom you seek." And he led them to Samaria. When they entered Samaria, Elisha said, "LORD, open the eyes of these men so that they may see." The LORD

opened their eyes, and they saw that there they were inside Samaria.
(2 Kings 6:17-20)

In this example, the opening of the eyes is God's doing, and with surprising results. With the "closed" eye, the servant was blind to see God's forces outnumbering an earthly king's, but not so with the "opened" eye. But there is a greater surprise to see: the narrative does not recount a conquest by "chariots of fire." Instead, God's chariots are there stationed on the mountain, and the Arameans themselves are struck with blindness, helplessly led into the capital city, where they could be easily slaughtered. Imagine their fright when their eyes are opened only to discover that they are now surrounded within the city of their enemy. But no slaughter is allowed. Instead, a banquet is served, and they depart with their stomachs full (6:22-23). Mission accomplished. There is more than meets the eye, and what meets the opened eye is always surprising, for better or worse.

There are a lot of "openings" in Luke's account of the Emmaus trek: the eyes, the Scriptures, and the mind (21:31, 32, 45). Each opening marks a delicate balance between knowledge and mystery. A simple act of sharing food becomes the vehicle of a dramatic revelation. Yet the resurrected Christ cannot be captured by sight. Literally, 24:31 reads, "Then their eyes were opened, and they recognized him; and he became invisible [*aphantos egeneto*] to them." Scientists tell us that light visible to the naked eye constitutes only a narrow slice of the electromagnetic spectrum, which consists of radio waves at one end and gamma rays at the other. Such extremes lie beyond human visibility, but they are perceived in other ways. Even more broadly, there is so much more to reality than can be captured by the periodic table, which lists every known chemical element in terms of its atomic structure. But all that is a mere slice of what is out there and around us, only three percent of all reality: dark energy and dark matter (and God knows what else) constitute everything else. Invisibility, in other words, in no way implies nonexistence. Jesus' disappearance at the table does not imply that Jesus abandoned the disciples. His "vanishing," rather, implies a different mode of presence. Call it a spectrally unlimited presence. Or call it spiritual.

In sum, a stranger "opens" the Scriptures to two disciples whose minds are closed. While they lack understanding, their sense of wonder begins to stir, wonder that prepares them for the culminating scene that triggers their recognition: sharing a meal with all eyes on the host. There at the table their eyes are "opened" long enough to recognize Jesus. "They did not see him" in the tomb (24:24); now they do not see him at the table (24:31). Nevertheless, it is in the "breaking of the bread" that Jesus was "made known" (24:34). Jesus remains invisibly present. The tomb is empty, but the table is not. In this episode, the Scriptures are not sufficient for recognizing Jesus, otherwise they would have prompted the disciples' recognition of Jesus as he expounded them. But the Scriptures in consort with a shared meal, a meal hosted by a stranger, make it possible. By opening the Scriptures, Jesus "opened their minds to understand them" (24:45). The walk to Emmaus is about opening eyes, ears, and hearts. It is also about opening the mouth. "There is nothing better" than to take and eat, to taste and see.

Invisible Matters

Luke's mysterious episode reminds me of Paul's bold statement: "We walk by faith, not by sight" (2 Cor. 5:7). But Paul does not mean to walk blindly. There is, in fact, much that we do that is not governed by what is directly visible. We do not live by sight alone. Some things that powerfully shape our lives are invisible. Like dark matter and dark energy, we see their effects on us and around us, but we do not see or touch their essence. What, for example, does justice look like? We know justice by the works of justice, by its tangible effects on people's lives. So also love and mercy. They are not things that can be ontologically analyzed, tested in labs, or sold in malls. They resist commodification. We know them, rather, by their effects, by their fruits, by what is done in their name. And yet we count them as real, necessarily so. The wonder of the resurrected Christ vanishing at the table opens my eyes to the wonder of those "invisible" things that govern my life, making them all the more real, as I walk by faith *and* by sight. It is in the "breaking of the bread" that Jesus is "made known." It is in the act of love that love is known.

16. Consummated Wonder

Behold, I am making all things new.

Revelation 21:5

Revelation (not "Revelations") is perhaps the most feared book in Scripture, and for good reason. Full of violent visions, strange symbolism, and cryptic images, this final book of the Bible is also the Bible's most perplexing. As its original (Greek) title indicates, the book announces the "Apocalypse" *(apokalypsis)*. In today's usage, that word conjures images of abject terror, such as the Four Horsemen (which are in Revelation) and Ichabod Crane (who is not). There is, of course, the iconic scene from Francis Ford Coppola's classic movie *Apocalypse Now,* in which the jungles of Vietnam erupt in fire at the music of the Doors ("The End"), after which the colonel played by Robert Duvall muses, "I love the smell of napalm in the morning; it smells like victory."

But the word "apocalypse" has nothing to do with napalm; it comes from the Greek verb *apokalyptein,* which simply means to "uncover" or "reveal," hence the English title "Revelation." Yet what the book reveals exactly is not at all clear. Revelation is, to be sure, all about revealing the events leading up to God's new reign on earth, but it does so in heavily coded language. Imparting knowledge while sustaining mystery, this book conceals as much as it reveals.

Knowledge of the book's historical background is essential for understanding something of its issues and concerns. Written toward the end of the reign of the Roman emperor Domitian (81-96 C.E.), Revelation was circulated as a letter to various congregations, specifically seven in Asia Minor. Each church is featured in a separate section in the letter. The author ("John") remains shrouded in mystery. All we know is that he was exiled to the tiny island of Patmos in the South Aegean, where he received his various visions. John lived in a time of conflict and potential persecution throughout the Roman Empire. The problem with the churches, according to John, was their accommodation to Roman culture and, in varying degrees, to imperial religion. John's visionary letter was a call to resist the temptation to assimilate, socially and religiously, to the empire and to "come screaming out of the Christian closet,"[1] knowing full well that the consequence could be death, but also knowing full well that death was no match for the glorious destiny to come.

New Heaven and New Earth

In the penultimate chapter of Revelation, John sees "a new heaven and a new earth" in which God descends to earth for the sake of creation's transformation. John, the exiled visionary, says this:

> Then I saw a new heaven and a new earth; for the first heaven and the first earth had passed away, and the sea was no longer there. And I saw the holy city, the new Jerusalem, coming down out of heaven from God, prepared as a bride adorned for her husband. And I heard a loud voice from the throne saying, "See, God's home [*he skene tou theou*] is with mortals. He will dwell [*skenosei*] with them; they will be his peoples, and God's very self will be with them." (21:2-3)

This is, as Barbara Rossing aptly calls it, a "rapture in reverse": God is raptured *down* to earth; God comes home to dwell on earth.[2] The language is not unfamiliar: it echoes the description of Christ's incarnation in the Gospel of John: "The Word became flesh and dwelled/made his home/moved into the neighborhood/tabernacled [*eskenosen*] among us" (John

---

1. Brian K. Blount, *Revelation: A Commentary,* New Testament Library (Louisville: Westminster John Knox, 2009), 13.
2. Barbara R. Rossing, *The Rapture Exposed: The Message of Hope in the Book of Revelation* (New York: Westview, 2004), 141-58.

1:14; see also Col. 1:19). The apocalypse is the final, cosmic event of God setting up shop "among us," of God taking up permanent residence on earth. It is incarnation taken to a new level, that of *cosmic* indwelling. It is resurrection taken to a new level, that of *cosmic* transformation. Jesus' resurrection as the "firstfruits" (1 Cor. 15:20, 23) leads to the resurrection of all creation, the final fruits.

Contrary to popular opinion (and a multibillion-dollar entertainment industry), there is no rapture in the book of Revelation.[3] The faithful do not ascend to heaven while the rest are left behind, consigned to destruction along with the planet. To the contrary, the holy city *descends;* God's heavenly habitation comes down to earth. The Apocalypse is not about departure, much less abandonment, but all about arrival and setting down permanent roots. In John's vision, earth accommodates heaven, and when that takes place, pain and suffering, death and decay — the marks of the old creation — will indeed pass away.

John's view of the new creation has a down-home distinctly urban focus. The new creation takes the form of a city, but not just any city. It is Jerusalem, the city of God (Pss. 46 and 48). The Jerusalem of antiquity was the place where God's tabernacle was finally established by David (2 Sam. 6) and where Solomon built a temple to enshrine God's presence on a more permanent basis (1 Kings 6-8). But in the end times, something dramatically changes: a new level of relationship is reached between God and God's people. The holy city is likened to a "bride adorned for her husband" (Rev. 21:2). It was biblical convention to describe cities as feminine, such as the oft-repeated designation "daughter Zion" (e.g., Ps. 9:14; Isa. 1:8; 10:32; 16:1; 52:2; 62:11; Jer. 6:23). In Isaiah, Jerusalem/Zion is also likened to a mother giving birth (Isa. 66:7-11). In Revelation, Jerusalem and "her" God find their consummation in the new creation. God's holy habitation descends to earth. The city awaits "as a bride" for God to enter her (Rev. 21:4). The holy city, and by extension all creation, is now God's home (21:3). The end mirrors the beginning, recalling Genesis 1's view of creation as God's cosmic sanctuary (see chapter 1).

---

3. Popular notions of the rapture are also based on false interpretations of 1 Thess. 4:13-17 and Matt. 24:36-44. In the first passage, Paul states that the "dead in Christ" will rise first to meet Jesus "in the air," followed by those still living, as Jesus *descends* to earth, not to join Jesus to ascend back up to heaven. In Matt. 24, as the flood swept away everyone except Noah's family, so being left behind, rather than being "taken up," is a good thing! See Rossing, *Rapture Exposed,* 174-84; and D. Mark Davis, *Left Behind and Loving It: A Cheeky Look at the End Times* (Eugene, OR: Cascade Books, 2011), 24-26.

By settling in the new city, God renews the covenant, which now extends beyond Israel to include all "mortals" (Rev. 21:3). Perhaps that is why John insists that the city will never be shut, for the city now welcomes all to enter through "her" gates (21:25). And as God's covenant is extended to all, so all suffering, including death, is "no more" (21:4). John's vision of the new creation is nothing short of staggering, for it marks nothing less than the coupling of heaven and earth. With the descent of the holy city, heaven itself has come to rest upon the earth. Heaven and earth have become one, and some things are no longer needed: the sea, the temple, the sun and moon, all replaced by God's radiant, life-giving presence (21:22-23). The reason the sea is singled out is because from John's perspective the sea connotes chaos, specifically the chaos of rebellion against God (e.g., 13:1). It is where the monsters of Rome and Babylon reside; it is the source of their imperial power. And so this "sea" has no place in the new creation (21:1). So also the night: no more darkness, for God's glory will provide uninterrupted light, God's glory whose light is the Lamb, the crucified Christ (21:23). The joy of consummation is enduring, without interruption.

One might think that with the city taking center stage in John's apocalyptic vision the garden with its flowing rivers is also no longer needed either (Gen. 2:8-14). By no means! In the sea's place is the "water of life," a river flowing from God's throne through the city:

> The angel showed me the river of the water of life, splendid as crystal, flowing from the throne of God and of the Lamb through the middle of the street of the city. On each side of the river are the trees[4] of life with their twelve kinds of fruit, producing their fruit each month; and the leaves of the trees are for the healing of the nations. (Rev. 22:1-2; cf. Ps. 46:4)

What John sees is a garden in the city. And along the river's banks flourish the *trees* of life! And with these trees are healing leaves for the nations. For John, the new creation is an urban garden whose political scope is cosmically international. Garden and city, Eden and Jerusalem, have merged, and in this urban Eden the tree of life in Genesis is cultivated into a veritable forest in Revelation. John's vision of the new Jerusalem "out-Edens" Eden itself![5]

---

4. Here the singular word "tree" is used collectively in Greek to designate a grove or forest.

5. Blount, *Revelation*, 397.

God and creation, heaven and earth, city and garden: John's vision of the end times is all about merging, about the cohabitation of the divine and the earthly. The driving force behind the new creation is perhaps best summed up with the divine declaration in 21:5. "Behold, I am making all things new" (cf. Isa. 43:19). God does *not* say, I am making all new things.[6] In the new creation, God is not starting all over again, creating from nothing after everything has been destroyed. It is not God's intent to leave earth behind. Indeed, there is only one place in Revelation in which God's wrath is affirmed in all its destructive potential: "Your wrath has come, and the time for judging the dead, . . . and for destroying those who destroy the earth" (11:18).

Those whom God consigns to destruction are themselves the destroyers of creation! They stand in the way of creation's restoration and renewal. It is not in God's plan to destroy creation, but to renew it, making possible God's final, complete turn toward earth, once and for all. It is consummation, not annihilation. God's creative work is all about making new, and the apocalypse marks the final, culminating work of renewal. Creation does not get eliminated in God's new work; it gets transformed. And as God's stewards of creation, we are enlisted to welcome creation's renewal by planting hope and pointing to signs of the new creation. As John sees it, creation's consummation is no fiery destruction but a flourishing garden in a peaceful city, an urban garden. That is "Apocalypse Now."

6. Blount, *Revelation,* 376-77.

Called to Wonder

The event of wonder is the original conversion.

Jerome A. Miller[1]

My ancestors were farmers. They had little time to "go marveling" except when it came time to take the very occasional trip to visit family on the other side of the country for a wedding or a funeral, or to visit their grandkids. My paternal grandparents raised their crops, from potatoes to alfalfa, in the Yakima Valley of Washington State. My grandmother moved there from Virginia to teach elementary school on the Yakima reservation and decided to stay after falling in love with my grandfather, a farmer. Although they did not regularly take strolls together on Sunday afternoons, my grandparents did marvel at each other's company at the dinner table, where family and friends were always welcomed.

Ben Olney, a Native American, was one such friend. The story goes that as an accomplished musician Ben enjoyed riding his horse on moonlit nights throughout the Simcoe Hills playing his violin. On one occasion he inadvertently rode into a sheep camp. The sheepherders panicked over the sound of eerie music in the dead of night, thinking that judgment day had arrived. Years later Ben became afflicted with arthritis and quit playing, but after his wife died he picked up the violin again and gradually regained

---

1. Jerome A. Miller, *In the Throe of Wonder: Intimations of the Sacred in a Post-Modern World* (Albany: SUNY Press, 1992), 175.

his ability. Ben would occasionally stop by my grandparents' place and stay for dinner. My grandfather enjoyed reminiscing with him about early life on the reservation, and my grandmother would make him promise to bring his violin the next time he came by. Conveniently, Ben would always forget. Nevertheless, the door remained open for Ben to invite himself in and eat, and my grandmother never lost hope that someday he would remember his violin and play it at the dinner table. But her hunger for wonder was never satisfied.

Wonder and Hope

The Bible satisfies our desire for wonder in a rich variety of ways: through arresting words, poetic subtleties, evocative images, glorious visions, hidden connections, narrative twists, provocative ambiguities, and generative paradoxes, to name a few. Capturing such wonder does not come about by skimming the text or searching for answers to a specific set of questions. Rather, the kind of wonder the Bible arouses is best experienced by reading the text with care and curiosity, with inquiry and deep respect, and that means pondering the text without pressing it into preconceived agendas. Reading with wonder is reading with expectancy but without a specific set of expectations, like reading a story for the first time. Reading with wonder, moreover, is dialogical: it involves a readiness to question the text and, equally so, a willingness to be questioned by the text. In wonder, the textual other and the textual reader are caught up in the act of sharing. Reading in dialogue with the text, moreover, places the reader in dialogue with others. Reading with wonder is reading in communion.

A Taxonomy of Tremendum

Wonder in the Bible, as we have seen, wears many faces. The various "texts of *tremendum*" discussed cover a wide range. Together they offer, one might say, a taxonomy or catalogue of wonder: sensational, mundane, and ontological wonder. But a whole other set of qualities highlights wonder's wild variety: playful, fearful, joyful, erotic, visionary, ordinary, surprising, orderly, puzzling, perplexing, unsettling, convicting. And it is no wonder that most of these texts have something to do with creation, each one offering its own shade of green . . . or red or brown or any other color that is sustainable and natural to a given landscape, as I am reminded by Terry Tempest Williams.[2] Wonder has its variety of contexts: cosmic temple and lush garden, rugged wilderness and cosmic playhouse, beautiful bodies and broken bread, fiery mountains and burning bushes, gushing streams and towering cedars, exotic beasts and one's own precious child. Throughout these texts, creation is both self-sustaining and contingent, firmly established and under construction, resilient and fragile, vital and volatile, stormy and settled, threatening and inspiring, old and new. In one way or another, a text's wonder points to creation's wonder.

A Network of Tremendum

A text's wonder also points to other texts. Connections abound within such a diverse array scattered throughout Scripture, and discovering them is part of the textual exercise of wonder. By placing texts next to each other, a dialogue filled with wonderings is bound to emerge. Take, for example, Noah's flood in Genesis and Christ's crucifixion in Mark, two quite disparate stories. Does God's decision to disarm unilaterally after the flood, signified by the bow hanging in the sky, find a connection with Jesus' giving up his life by hanging on the cross? Or the Song of Songs and the book of Revelation: does the deep yearning for union between two lovers in a lush garden have anything to do with God's passionate longing to be at home in creation? Does Wisdom playing in creation (Prov. 8) have something to do with God reconciling the world in Christ (John 1)? What about Christ's incarnation and God's "rapture in reverse"? How about the wonder of a simple meal in Ecclesiastes and the eucharistic moment of recognition in Luke? The wellspring of textual dialogue is inexhaustible. The Bible is an intertextual wonderland.

An Itinerary of Tremendum

What happens, moreover, when we place certain texts in some sequential order? Nothing short of a drama unfolds, a journey of wonder that proceeds from creation to cross to new creation, a story of beginnings and new beginnings. As a whole, the Bible bears witness to God's ongoing *Cosmos* Project,

2. See Terry Tempest Williams, *Red: Passion and Patience in the Desert* (New York: Vintage, 2002), esp. 133-40.

within which is nested God's *Homo* Project.[3] Both "projects" are inseparably connected. Indeed, the latter is very much a part of the former, and both are subsumed under a grand narrative arc from Genesis to Revelation that charts God's *Homecoming* Project. This unfolding drama begins with creating and concludes with indwelling. It begins with reaching out and letting go and moves toward drawing near and entering in, without ever letting go. It is God's story, our story, earth's story. It is the story of creation and communion, yearning and consummation. That's the Big Picture I see.

As the drama unfolds, I also see woven together two "sides" of God, divine polarities that, it turns out, attract rather than repel: (1) the transcendent God of power and might and (2) the immanent God of *eros* and intimacy. Throughout the Bible, we discover the God of great and small wonders, the God of mighty acts and minor acts. There's the elusive God, and there's the alluring God, the almighty God and the all-loving God, the God who is infinite and the God who becomes finite, the God of Glory and the God of glory, the magnificent and the mundane. These various aspects, inseparable as they are (and admittedly painted with far too broad brush strokes), are set together, side by side, "in the beginning," within the first two chapters of Genesis: God the cosmic king and God the dirty farmer. One constructs a temple and the other plants a garden. So the drama begins.

"In the beginning" there was God alone in the dark, in darkness pregnant with potential. Then in one stroke of breath God unleashed light and from there fashioned a world vibrant with life in all its many hues. An unexpected universe! As God fashioned a world in collaboration, so a world is fashioned for companionship and community, for order and for intimacy. God creates a creating world, a living temple, a sustainable world set free to flourish and to suffer. In Sabbath, God lets go to let creation have its freedom: so far so "good" until the world nearly destroys itself. The cosmic temple is cast in ruins because the "image of God" has forsaken its identity and purpose. By all appearances it seems that God has created a monstrosity, the monstrosity of "man," thanks to the human tendency to transgress boundaries, to twist "dominion" into domination, partnership into competition, receiving into taking and hoarding. So violence engulfs the world, and God's cosmic house becomes a den of murderers.

But far from abandoning creation, God seeks to cleanse the world of its violence while preserving its rich diversity. God hits the "reset button," but the results are mixed. Humanity doesn't change, not fundamentally at

---

3. *Homo sapiens* for now.

least, but God does! God resolves never again to resort to destroying life in order to (re)create life. Such is the basis of God's first covenant, a cosmic covenant no less, a self-restraining order established to preserve the freedom of life, human and otherwise. By hanging up the bow, the divine warrior renounces violence in hope that humanity would do the same. But it is not enough: it is only the first move in God's disarming love for the world.

God seeks a more intimate relationship. So God cultivates a community. "I will be their God and they shall be my people," says God — a covenant code aimed at sustaining a new community, a community founded in freedom and built on justice as a "light to the nations" (Isa. 42:6). A law is born, and so also a people. In God, law and salvation, testimony and *torah*, become part of a seamless whole, the wholeness of *shalom,* in the life of a community, in life together. This newly constituted people is the least among the nations but the most treasured in God's eyes. Within this developing relationship, God becomes ever more self-revealing, ever more emergent in word and presence. To Moses, God shares God's very heart: filled with mercy and grace, slow to anger, passionate in faithful love, ready to forgive, and poised for justice (Exod. 34:6-7). Such is God's self-confession.

But even that proves insufficient. So prophets are called to convey God's pathos, God's agonizing *eros* for grace and justice. As Israel was least among the nations, so the least within Israel are to receive special consideration and care, justice on their behalf. God's love is to be practiced locally in care for the poor and needy, systemically in the cause of justice for the least, and ecologically for the sake of creation. Injustice committed within the beloved community, the prophets proclaimed, is directly felt within the larger biotic community. The earth mourns and languishes, the land lies polluted, "waste and void," all because of human neglect and violation of God's covenantal norms (Hos. 4:1-3; Isa. 24:4; Jer. 4:24-26). The fate of the least and the fate of the earth are inseparably linked, the prophets point out. So stop and smell the dead fish and ponder (Hos. 4:3).

But words alone, however prophetic or poetic, cannot change the hardened heart. So God chooses to create again, this time by putting flesh into the fray, God's very own. In Christ, God formally enters into creation, into the finitude and frailty of life. In Christ, God becomes Emmanuel, "God with us," body and soul, God with the world, beloved and biotic. In Christ, God comes as an infant crying in a manger, as a healer who gets exhausted, as a teacher who gets exasperated, as a criminal hanging on the cross, as the "Word made flesh." In Christ, the creator becomes created; the creator of all becomes the creature for all. In Christ, the disarmed God, the Lamb, comes to disarm the powers that wreak destruction and keep the outcast cast out. Like Job keeping company in the wild, Jesus spends his time with the poor and sick, with women and lepers, with demoniacs and tax collectors, sinners and Samaritans, the least and the despised. And he is always moving, eliciting surprise along the way: healing, freeing, confronting, comforting, overturning, reconciling. Unlike Wisdom, who builds her house of seven pillars, beckoning all who pass by to enter (Prov. 9:1-2), Christ goes out and about, homeless in the world. Always going "ahead" (Mark 16:7), Jesus refuses to be pinned down. More than a prophet, more than a teacher, more than a liberal or a conservative, Jesus is the Messiah on the move, breaking molds and transgressing limits. For Jesus, restoring relationships knows no bounds or boundaries. "In him all things hold together" (Col. 1:17).

But Jesus allows himself to be nailed down. The story of the Bible is the drama of God who becomes vulnerable in the flesh to the point of death. The cross is the defining moment in which God's credibility with the world reaches its greatest height. The cross is the scar of God's love for the world, the wound of Emmanuel in the flesh. Through the wound of the cross, itself a symbol of atrocity, God can no longer be called indifferent to the human cry and to creation's grave groaning. From cross to tomb, God's descent into the depths of creation's "bondage to decay" marks the beginning of creation's liberation for healing and renewal. *On* the cross, sin is absorbed and violence taken in. *From* the cross, sin is transformed into forgiveness and violence turned to reconciliation. From the cross, life emerges from death, the womb from the tomb, the new creation from the old. And it all begins, once again, in the dark. The empty tomb is emptied of death and filled with the light of life. An unexpected resurrection! An unexpected new creation that points to a world replenished with everlasting life on that day when God settles permanently on earth, never to let go, never to leave behind. That is the day when Sabbath holds final sway, the day of unending rest and enduring wonder. The Bible dramatizes the journey of God's ever expanding love, from Jews to Gentiles to the earth and all therein, a love already established "in the beginning." It is also the journey of God's ever deepening, ever riskier love, a love that takes God from king to gardener to groundling, even unto death. And so it is that the Bible is a journey filled with "painful wrenchings and surprising gifts," including God's.[4] God's story, our story, creation's story: whether in the

---

4. Walter Brueggemann, "Covenanting as Human Vocation: The Relation of the Bible

eyes of the believer or in the ears of the skeptic, a story of this magnitude, a story of such paradox and poignancy, of mystery both magisterial and mundane, is indeed something to wonder about.

Welcoming Wonder

But one might ask of all this: So what? Is experiencing the wonder and mystery of the biblical drama simply an end in itself, something simply to be enjoyed and pondered? More broadly, is there something more to wonder than the occasional shooting star or textual discovery or dramatic telling? Is wonder sustainable? Can it be cultivated? Can wonder lead to new orientation?

It all depends. There's always an element of choice involved in welcoming wonder. By way of illustration, philosopher Jerome Miller lifts up the archetypal childhood experience of discovering a door to a secret room. The child can do one of three things. She can flee, frightened by what may be lurking on the other side, sensing that she is on forbidden ground. Or she can "stand motionless" before the door, transfixed and pondering. Or she may get "the courage to raise her hand toward the latch," however hesitatingly.[5] "Wonder puts into motion precisely this dreadful play between withdrawal and venturing, retreat and longing, reluctance and urgency, delay and hastening."[6] Although she is held in the grip of "fascination and terror,"[7] it is the sway of wonder that prompts her to venture forth, rather than turn back, and open the door. As Miller admits but does not fully develop, to enter fully into wonder takes courage. To welcome wonder is to muster the courage to risk change.

Waiting with Wonder

To welcome wonder is also to linger in hope and live in anticipation, something that adults (at least some of them) can appreciate more than children. This is adultlike, rather than childlike, wonder; it is wonder matured. Much

and Pastoral Care," in *The Psalms and the Life of Faith,* ed. Patrick D. Miller (Minneapolis: Augsburg Fortress, 1995), 150-66 at 163.

5. Miller, *In the Throe of Wonder,* 36.

6. Miller, *In the Throe of Wonder,* 36.

7. Miller, *In the Throe of Wonder,* 35.

of wonder is found in the waiting, not just in the receiving, not simply in expectations fulfilled. Waiting with wonder is no passive exercise. It is hope filled, and that is precisely how the Bible ends its drama, leaving the reader waiting with great expectation, waiting with wonder for the new creation, praying unceasingly *maranatha*, "Come, Lord Jesus!" (Rev. 2:20; cf. 1 Cor. 16:22). Such waiting does not involve obsessing over (and predicting) the precise time of arrival. Waiting with wonder is comfortable with the unknown even as it remains ever restless with the known, dissatisfied with the way things are. The conclusion of the biblical drama is meant to leave the reader not in fear of judgment or in yearning for escape but in the wonder of renewal. Such is the lasting power of Revelation's book, the power to sustain our restless waiting, to sustain our watching for, and working toward, signs that indicate creation's renewal. And in the meantime, as we wait and work toward that end, hospitality is extended to strangers and friends (regardless of whether they've remembered their violins) to sit at table and to savor what is offered, a foretaste of God's coming kingdom. Wonder welcomes others as it waits on others.

To welcome wonder is also to behold the world as wondrous, resisting the urge to treat it only for its utility. It is one thing to see creation as a warehouse filled with commodities to be used for convenience and to enhance luxurious lifestyles. It is quite another to see it in relation to the mystery of God. It is our failure to wonder, I would submit, that is at the root of our planetary crisis. If we lose our sense of wonder, we lose the world and ourselves. But if we lose ourselves in wonder, then there's always hope.

Stewards of God's Mysteries

In his first letter to the church in Corinth, Paul says this about how he wants himself and his colleagues in ministry to be regarded:

> One should regard us in this way, as servants of Christ and stewards of God's mysteries. Now, it is required of stewards that they be found trustworthy. (1 Cor. 4:1-2)

"Stewards of God's mysteries." That effectively summarizes Paul's sense of call. What "mysteries" does Paul have in mind? No doubt everything from God's creation to Jesus' crucifixion and resurrection, to the birth of the church at Pentecost, to his own conversion and apostleship — all of it pointing to the new creation in Christ. Paul has in mind the whole litany of God's mighty and minor acts, including what the church boldly proclaims as the great mystery of faith: "Christ has died, Christ is risen, Christ will come again."

Paul is also adamant about "stewards" being "trustworthy." A trustworthy steward is one who both preserves and generously shares, one who is not in it only for the moment but is committed to abide in such a calling, to endure in wonder. Stewards of God's wonders are themselves practitioners of wonder, and practicing wonder begins with *seeing* in a new way, with seeing oneself and others as "fearfully and wonderfully made" (Ps. 139:14). Or as Paul says in another letter to the Corinthians, "from now on, therefore, we regard no one from a human point of view [*kata sarka*]" (2 Cor. 5:16). Paul goes on to say:

> Therefore, if anyone is in Christ, a new creation [*kaine ktisis*]! Everything old has passed away [*parerchomai*]. See, everything has become new [*kaina*]! (5:17)

To see the other as "new," as made in the "image of God," now in the image of Christ, is key to beholding the other in wonder. No wonder Paul moves immediately from this bold proclamation to unpacking the "ministry of reconciliation" (5:18). Reconciliation is itself a defining mark of the new creation, the cosmic follow-up to "seeing" in Christ.

Seeing and Watching

It all comes down to how one sees the other. It is what Andrew Sung Park says about the categorical difference between *seeing* and *watching*. "Seeing implies a warm intention, yielding constructive transformation," whereas "watching involves a biased look, engendering harmful consequences."[8] Whereas seeing allows for wonder, watching smacks of suspicion and prejudice. Seeing well, moreover, is the basis of community. "Seeing stands for visual dialogue and understanding, arousing sympathy; watching [stands]

---

8. Andrew Sung Park, "A Theology of Transmutation," in *A Dream Unfinished: Theological Reflections on America from the Margins,* ed. Eleazar S. Fernandez (Maryknoll, NY: Orbis, 2001), 152-66 at 158. My thanks to Marcia Riggs for bringing this essay to my attention.

for a visual monologue, yielding an unpleasant staring, cold look," the harsh, leering gaze.[9] As the tragic history of racism in America attests time and again, "watching" kills.[10] The "courage to have constructive images of others," Park goes on to say, "constitutes the strength of seeing."[11] It is the courage to reconcile and affiliate, the courage to resist fear and hatred, the courage to welcome the other in wonder. Yes, wonder has all to do with "the strength of seeing" and, thus, with the strength of being, of being in community. The wonder of each other draws each other together, as the face of Christ is seen in the face of the other — individual, social, and creational. The encompassing, holistic scope of wonder has to do not just with "spiritual formation" but with *nephesh* formation, with body-and-soul formation, with person and community, spirit and soil, character and creation.

Docents in the House of Wonder

As trustworthy "stewards of God's mysteries," we are called to wonder. Michael Jinkins suggestively recasts Paul's self-designated vocation as "docents in the house of wonder."[12] A docent works, for example, in a museum or in a cathedral and points out things that could be easily overlooked but are of great interest.[13] A docent adds depth to what can be seen and reveals things that are hard to see. A docent's responsibility is to guide, share background information, and uncover what is hidden — all to cultivate a sense of wonder about the place where people are standing, walking, and exploring. The docent transforms tourists into pilgrims.[14] That captures well how I see my role in relation to the biblical text: to invite readers to explore the text, to offer a modicum of background information, and most crucially to point out things in the text that I find particularly wondrous. An exegete is a "docent in the text of wonder," and the text of wonder is a window into the "house of the LORD," which for Jinkins is primarily the

9. Park, "A Theology of Transmutation," 158.

10. Recently confirmed in the shooting of Trayvon Martin, a seventeen-year-old African American high school student in Sanford, Florida, on February 12, 2012.

11. Park, "A Theology of Transmutation," 159.

12. Michael Jinkins, *The Church Transforming: What's Next for the Reformed Project?* (Louisville: Westminster John Knox, 2012), 83-88.

13. Jinkins, *The Church Transforming,* 86.

14. Jinkins, *The Church Transforming,* 85.

church. But as our various texts of *tremendum* make clear, God's "house" is far more capacious. It is more than the church, more than the temple. Thanks to Genesis and Revelation, the "house of the LORD" is God's cosmic sanctuary.[15]

Wonder is a calling. It is our calling in and for God's changing world. It calls forth courage to face our deepest fears and to shape our deepest desires for good. Wonder opens us to Wisdom. Wonder calls us to disorientation, unsettling pathos that it is, and to new orientation.[16] If discovering a secret door is the deciding point of wonder, we can trust knowing full well who stands on the other side, beckoning us to open it:

> Behold! I stand at the door and knock; if you hear my voice and open the door, I will come in to you and eat with you, and you with me. (Rev. 3:20)

---

15. There is, in fact, no temple in the new creation, according to Revelation (21:22). That would also apply to church.

16. The functional categories formulated by Walter Brueggemann in *The Message of the Psalms: A Theological Commentary* (Minneapolis: Augsburg, 1984) — orientation, disorientation, and new orientation or reorientation — are applicable in so many ways. As I argue, they lie at the heart of wonder's movement. See also Mary-Jane Rubenstein, *Strange Wonder: The Closure of Metaphysics and the Opening of Awe,* Insurrections: Critical Studies in Religion, Politics, and Culture (New York: Columbia University Press, 2008), 60.

Works Cited

Ball, Phillip. *Curiosity: How Science Became Interested in Anything.* Chicago: University of Chicago Press, 2012.

Barth, Karl. *Dogmatics in Outline.* Translated by G. T. Thomson. London: SCM, 1959.

———. *Evangelical Theology: An Introduction.* New York: Holt, Rinehart & Winston, 1963.

———. "The Fear of the Lord Is the Beginning of Wisdom." *Interpretation* 14 (1960): 433-39.

Beerling, David. *The Emerald Planet: How Plants Changed Earth's History.* Oxford: Oxford University Press, 2007.

Blount, Brian K. *Invasion of the Dead: Preaching Resurrection.* Louisville: Westminster John Knox, 2014.

———. *Revelation: A Commentary.* New Testament Library. Louisville: Westminster John Knox, 2009.

Bonhoeffer, Dietrich. *Creation and Fall: A Theological Interpretation of Genesis 1–3: Temptation.* Translated by John C. Fletcher. London: SCM, 1959.

Brand, Stewart. *Whole Earth Discipline: An Ecopragmatist Manifesto.* New York: Viking, 2009.

Brown, William P. *The Seven Pillars of Creation: The Bible, Science, and the Ecology of Wonder.* New York: Oxford University Press, 2010.

———. *Structure, Role, and Ideology in the Hebrew and Greek Texts of Genesis 1:1–2:3.* Society of Biblical Literature Dissertation Series 132. Atlanta: Scholars Press, 1993.

———. *Wisdom's Wonder: Character, Creation, and Crisis in the Bible's Wisdom Literature.* Grand Rapids: Eerdmans, 2014.

Brueggemann, Walter. "The Book of Jeremiah: Portrait of the Prophet." *Interpretation* 37 (1983): 130-45.

———. "Covenanting as Human Vocation: The Relation of the Bible and Pastoral Care." Pages 150-66 in *The Psalms and the Life of Faith.* Edited by Patrick D. Miller. Minneapolis: Augsburg Fortress, 1995.

———. *The Message of the Psalms: A Theological Commentary.* Minneapolis: Augsburg, 1984.

———. "Of the Same Flesh and Bone [Gen 2,23a]." *Catholic Biblical Quarterly* 32 (1970): 532-42.

———. *The Prophetic Imagination.* 2nd edition. Minneapolis: Fortress, 2001.

Bulkeley, Kelly. *The Wondering Brain: Thinking about Religion with and beyond Cognitive Neuroscience.* New York: Routledge, 2005.

Calvin, John. *Commentary on the Book of Psalms,* vol. 6. Translated by James Anderson. Grand Rapids: Baker, 1979.

Campbell, Mary Bruce. *Wonder and Science: Imagining Worlds in Early Modern Europe.* Ithaca: Cornell University Press, 1999.

Carson, Rachel L. *The Sense of Wonder.* New York: HarperCollins, 1998.

Craddock, Fred B. *Craddock Stories.* Edited by Mike Graves and Richard F. Ward. St. Louis: Chalice, 2001.

Dalley, Stephanie. *Myths from Mesopotamia: Creation, the Flood, Gilgamesh, and Others.* World's Classics. Oxford: Oxford University Press, 1991.

Daston, Lorraine, and Katherine Park. *Wonders and the Order of Nature.* New York: Zone, 1998.

Davis, D. Mark. *Left Behind and Loving It: A Cheeky Look at the End Times.* Eugene, OR: Cascade, 2011.

Davis, Ellen F. *Proverbs, Ecclesiastes, and the Song of Songs.* Westminster Bible Companion. Louisville: Westminster John Knox, 2000.

Dawkins, Richard. *Unweaving the Rainbow: Science, Delusion, and the Appetite for Wonder.* New York: Houghton Mifflin, 1998.

Deane-Drummond, Celia. *Wonder and Wisdom: Conversations in Science, Spirituality, and Theology.* Philadelphia: Templeton Foundation, 2006.

Einstein, Albert. "The World as I See It." Translated by Sonja Bargmann. Pages 8-11 in *Ideas and Opinions, Based on* Mein Weltbild. Edited by Carl Seelig. New York: Crown, 1954 [orig. 1931].

Exum, J. Cheryl. *Song of Songs.* Old Testament Library. Louisville: Westminster John Knox, 2005.

Fewell, Danna N., and David M. Gunn. "Shifting the Blame: God in the Garden."

Pages 16-33 in *Reading Bibles, Writing Bodies: Identity and the Book.* Edited by Timothy K. Beal and David M. Gunn. London: Routledge, 1997.

Fox, Michael V. "'*Āmôn* Again." *Journal of Biblical Literature* 115 (1996): 699-702.

Fuller, Robert C. *Wonder: From Emotion to Spirituality.* Chapel Hill: University of North Carolina Press, 2006.

González-Andrieu, Cecilia. *Bridge to Wonder: Art as a Gospel of Beauty.* Waco: Baylor University Press, 2012.

Goodenough, Ursula. *The Sacred Depths of Nature.* Oxford: Oxford University Press, 1998.

Gregersen, Niels Henrik. "Deep Incarnation: Why Evolutionary Continuity Matters in Christology." *Toronto Journal of Theology* 26 (2010): 173-88.

Griffin, Ralph C., III. "The Subversive Sage: Qoheleth and the Praxis of Resistance." Th.M. thesis. Decatur, GA: Columbia Theological Seminary, 2014.

Gussow, Mel. "For Saul Bellow, Seeing the Earth with Fresh Eyes." *New York Times* (26 May 1997). Accessed 17 September 2012 at http://www.nytimes .com/1997/05/26/books/for-saul-bellow-seeing-the-earth-with-fresh-eyes .html?scp=1&sq=Gussow%20%22Seeing%20the%20Earth%22&st=cse.

Heschel, Abraham Joshua. *God in Search of Man: A Philosophy of Judaism.* New York: Farrar, Straus & Giroux, 1955.

———. *The Prophets,* vol. 1. New York: Harper, 1969.

Holmes, Richard. *The Age of Wonder: How the Romantic Generation Discovered the Beauty and Terror of Science.* New York: Vintage, 2010.

Holmstedt, Robert D. "The Restrictive Syntax of Genesis i 1." *Vetus Testamentum* 58 (2008): 56-67.

Hundley, Michael B. *Gods in Dwellings: Temples and Divine Presence in the Ancient Near East.* Writings from the Ancient World Supplement Series 3. Atlanta: Society of Biblical Literature, 2013.

Impey, Chris. *The Living Cosmos: Our Search for Life in the Universe.* New York: Random, 2007.

James, E. L. *Fifty Shades of Grey.* New York: Vintage, 2012.

Jinkins, Michael. *The Church Transforming: What's Next for the Reformed Project?* Louisville: Westminster John Knox, 2012.

Jones, Scott C. "Corporeal Discourse in the Book of Job." *Journal of Biblical Literature* 132 (2013): 845-63.

Jones, Serene. *Trauma and Grace: Theology in a Ruptured World.* Louisville: Westminster John Knox, 2009.

Juel, Donald. "Christian Hope and the Denial of Death: Encountering New Testament Eschatology." Pages 171-83 in *The End of the World and the Ends of*

God: Science and Theology on Eschatology. Edited by John Polkinghorne and Michael Welker. Harrisburg, PA: Trinity, 2000.

Keen, Sam. *Apology for Wonder.* New York: Harper & Row, 1969.

Konner, Melvin. *The Tangled Wing: Biological Constraints on the Human Spirit.* 2nd edition. New York: Henry Holt, 2002.

Krüger, Thomas. *Qoheleth: A Commentary.* Translated by O. C. Dean Jr. Edited by K. Baltzer. Hermeneia. Minneapolis: Fortress, 2004.

Lamott, Anne. *Help, Thanks, Wow: The Three Essential Prayers.* New York: Riverhead, 2012.

Lauterbach, Jacob Z., ed. *Mekhilta de-Rabbi Ishmael,* vol. 2. Philadelphia: Jewish Publication Society, 2004.

McBride, S. Dean, Jr. "Divine Protocol: Genesis 1:1–2:3 as Prologue to the Pentateuch." Pages 3-41 in *God Who Creates: Essays in Honor of W. Sibley Towner.* Edited by William P. Brown and S. Dean McBride Jr. Grand Rapids: Eerdmans, 2000.

McCary, P. K. *Black Bible Chronicles,* vol. 1: *From Genesis to the Promised Land.* New York: African American Family, 1993.

Merton, Thomas. *Raids on the Unspeakable.* New York: New Directions, 1964.

Meyers, Carol. " 'To Her Mother's House': Considering a Counterpart to the Israelite *Bêt 'āb.*" Pages 39-51 in *Bible and the Politics of Exegesis: Essays in Honor of Norman K. Gottwald on His Sixty-Fifth Birthday.* Edited by David Jobling et al. Cleveland: Pilgrim, 1991.

Miller, Jerome A. *In the Throe of Wonder: Intimations of the Sacred in a Post-Modern World.* Albany: SUNY Press, 1992.

Newsom, Carol A. "Genesis 2–3 and *1 Enoch* 6–16: Two Myths of Origin and Their Ethical Implications." Pages 7-22 in *Shaking Heaven and Earth: Essays in Honor of Walter Brueggemann and Charles B. Cousar.* Edited by Christine Roy Yoder et al. Louisville: Westminster John Knox, 2005.

Nussbaum, Martha C. *Upheavals of Thought: The Intelligence of Emotions.* New York: Cambridge University Press, 2001.

Otto, Rudolf. *The Idea of the Holy: An Inquiry into the Non-rational Factor in the Idea of the Divine and Its Relation to the Rational.* New York: Oxford University Press, 1958.

Park, Andrew Sung. "A Theology of Transmutation." Pages 152-66 in *A Dream Unfinished: Theological Reflections on America from the Margins.* Edited by Eleazar S. Fernandez. Maryknoll, NY: Orbis, 2001.

Parker, Julie Faith. "Blaming Eve Alone: Translation, Omission, and Implications of *'mh* in Genesis 3:6b." *Journal of Biblical Literature* 132 (2013): 729-47.

Phipps, William E. "Eve and Pandora Contrasted." *Theology Today* 45 (1988): 34-48.

Plato, *Theaetetus, Sophist.* Translated by Harold North Fowler. Loeb Classical Library. Cambridge: Harvard University Press, 1967.

Pope, Marvin H. *Song of Songs A New Translation with Introduction and Commentary.* Anchor Bible 7C. Garden City, NY: Doubleday, 1977.

Rivera, Mayra. "Glory: The First Passion of Theology?" Pages 167-85 in *Polydoxy: Theology of Multiplicity and Relation.* Edited by Catherine Keller and Laurel Schneider. New York: Routledge, 2011.

Rossing, Barbara R. *The Rapture Exposed: The Message of Hope in the Book of Revelation.* New York: Westview, 2004.

Rubenstein, Mary-Jane. *Strange Wonder: The Closure of Metaphysics and the Opening of Awe.* Insurrections: Critical Studies in Religion, Politics, and Culture. New York: Columbia University Press, 2008.

Scott, R. B. Y. "Wisdom in Creation: The *'Āmôn* of Proverbs viii 30." *Vetus Testamentum* 10 (1960): 213-23.

Smith, Mark S. *The Priestly Vision of Genesis 1.* Minneapolis: Fortress, 2010.

Smolin, Lee. *The Life of the Cosmos.* London: Phoenix, 1997.

Terrien, Samuel. *The Elusive Presence: Toward a New Biblical Theology.* Religious Perspectives 26. San Francisco: Harper & Row, 1978.

Towner, W. Sibley. "Ecclesiastes." Pages 265-360 in *New Interpreter's Bible,* volume 5. Edited by Leander Keck and Richard Clifford. Nashville: Abingdon, 1997.

Tuell, Steven S. "A Riddle Resolved by an Enigma: Hebrew *glš* and Ugaritic GLṮ." *Journal of Biblical Literature* 112 (1993): 99-104.

White, E. B. "Introduction." Pages xvii-xix in K. S. White's *Onward and Upward in the Garden.* Edited by E. B. White. New York: Farrar Straus Giroux/Toronto: McGraw-Hill Ryerson, 1979.

Williams, Terry Tempest. *Red: Passion and Patience in the Desert.* New York: Vintage, 2002.

Yadin, Azzan. "*Qôl* as Hypostasis in the Hebrew Bible." *Journal of Biblical Literature* 122 (2003): 601-26.

Subject and Name Index

Scripture Index